Wetlands

BY Pamela Hickman

ILLUSTRATED BY Judie Shore

FEDERATION OF
Ontario
Naturalists

Kids Can Press Ltd.
TORONTO

Kids Can Press Ltd. acknowledges with appreciation the assistance of the Canada Council and the Ontario Arts Council in the production of this book.

Canadian Cataloguing in Publication Data

Hickman, Pamela
    Wetlands

Includes index.
ISBN 1-55074-126-8

1. Wetlands – United States – Juvenile literature.
2. Wetlands – Canada – Juvenile literature.
3. Wetland conservation – Juvenile literature.
4. Wetland ecology – Juvenile literature.
5. Conservation of natural resources – Juvenile literature.
I. Shore, Judie.   II.Title.

QH541.5.M3H52 1993   j574.5'26325   C92-094066-8

93.06.24   LSC 10.95

Neither the publisher nor the author shall be liable for any damage which may be caused or sustained as a result of the conduct of any of the activities in this book, from not specifically following instructions or conducting the activities without proper supervision, or from ignoring the cautions contained in the text.

The Federation of Ontario Naturalists (FON) is a non-profit, membership organization that is committed to protecting and increasing awareness of important natural habitats, wilderness areas and endangered wildlife. The FON cooperates with national and international organizations to achieve these goals. For more information on the FON or how to become a member contact the Federation of Ontario Naturalists, 355 Lesmill Road, Don Mills, Ontario M3B 2W8, Phone (416)444-8419, Fax (416)444-9866.

Kids Can Press Ltd.
29 Birch Avenue
Toronto, Ontario, Canada
M4V 1E2

Edited by Laurie Wark
Designed by Michael Solomon
Typeset by Esperança Melo
Printed and bound in Canada

Text stock contains
over 50% recycled paper

93 0 9 8 7 6 5 4 3 2 1

Contents

Acknowledgements

The Federation of Ontario Naturalists (FON) has championed the cause of wetlands protection in Ontario for many decades. Their successes in achieving a wetlands policy in the province stemmed from the tireless dedication of many individuals and federated clubs. During my years on staff at the FON, I was inspired by the relentless determination and commitment to the cause of these special people: Mike Singleton, Ron Reid, Nancy Patterson, Arlin Hackman, Don Huff, Marion Taylor and Ian Kirkham.

I would like to thank Nancy Patterson, former Wetlands Specialist with the FON, for her assistance in reviewing the manuscript. I also owe Nancy a rather large debt from years ago — she hired me to write a Wetlands Education Kit for elementary schools in 1982. It was my first job as a writer and I've never looked back. Thanks, Nancy. In addition, I appreciate the help of Nancy Croome Makowski, Education Coordinator for FON, in reviewing the manuscript.

Thanks also go to Kids Can Press and my ever encouraging editor, Laurie Wark, who managed to keep everything together and on time despite my household move from Ontario to Nova Scotia in the middle of this book. Thank goodness for fax machines, too! A special note of thanks goes to Michael Solomon, our wonderful book designer.

To my sister, Jill Forbes – PH

To my sister, Coral – JS

What are Wetlands?

Where can you go to see moose and minnows, marsh wrens and muskrat? Where can you find a mat of moss or a collection of cattails? The answer is a wetland — also known as a pothole, slough, bayou, quagmire, muskeg, marsh, swamp, bog and fen. Whatever you call them, you'll discover that wetlands are amazing habitats where land and water meet. In this section you'll find out how to tell the difference between a marsh, swamp, fen and bog — the four basic types of wetlands covered in this book. Each one is an important habitat for a variety of plants and animals that are specially adapted to their waterlogged home. As well as teeming with life, wetlands reduce flooding and erosion and filter sediments and pollution from the water. Read on to find out how you can set up some simple experiments and see for yourself how wetlands make the environment a better place for everyone.

In this book, you'll find lots to do and explore. There are activities to do outdoors when you're visiting a wetland, or indoors back at home. You can even make some of your own discoveries by trying out the experiments.

Just watch for the symbols shown here to find out what kind of activity is coming up.

Remember to return all creatures safely to their wetland homes once you're finished observing them, and don't take anything from parks or nature reserves.

An activity:

TRY THIS!

An experiment:

EXPERIMENT!

Welcome to a wetland

What do moose, muskrat and marsh-marigolds have in common? They all live in wetlands, along with thousands of other plants and animals. Before you head out to look at the amazing assortment of life in a wetland, you'll need to know where to look. A wetland is — you guessed it — wet. Wetland soils are either full of water or underwater, and the plants that live in wetlands are adapted to growing in very wet conditions. You'll find wetlands along the shallow edges of rivers, streams, ponds, lakes and oceans, between dry land and deep water. Some wetlands also form in big hollows that were scooped out by glaciers thousands of years ago.

There are four basic types of wetlands: marsh, swamp, bog and fen. Wetlands are divided into these different kinds depending on where they are located, what kinds of plants grow in them and what kinds of soils they have. You can discover what kind of wetlands are in your area by doing a wetland test. Go through the checklists on the next few pages for a quick summary of each wetland type. Then grab your rubber boots, binoculars, bug net and sketch pad and get ready to explore a wet and wonderful world.

Marsh

If you see cattails, bulrushes and other soft-stemmed emergent plants that grow with their roots underwater and their stems and leaves above water, then you've found a marsh. Marshes can be knee-deep or over your head, that is, up to 2 m (7 feet) deep. Deep marshes have floating plants, such as water-lilies, and underwater plants, such as bladderwort. Freshwater marshes form along the shores of sheltered rivers and streams or in the shallows of ponds and lakes. They get their water from underground springs, streams that flow into them, rainfall and run-off from melting snow in the spring. Some freshwater marshes are found in shallow potholes, or sloughs (pronounced "slooz"), and only get water from run-off and rain. In dry periods, these shallow marshes may dry up completely. When spring flooding and rains return, the seeds that were dropped in the mud by last summer's plants grow, and the marsh comes back to life.

Along the sea coasts, saltwater marshes grow between the muddy tidal flats, which are left bare when the tide goes out, and the higher dry land. Twice a day these marshes are flooded and drained as the tide rolls in and out. The grasses and other tall plants that grow there are specially adapted to these constant changes in water level and temperature.

Marshes are home to a wide variety of wildlife, from the tiny plankton floating in the water to the huge moose that wade into the marsh in search of tasty water-lily roots. Animals who visit or live in marshes find food, shelter, a place to raise their young and protection from enemies and bad weather.

Marsh checklist

- soft-stemmed emergent plants growing with roots in the water and stems out of the water
- found along the shores of rivers, streams and coasts, or in the shallows of ponds or lakes. May also form in potholes, or sloughs.
- water from 15 cm to 2 m (6 inches to 7 feet) deep. Water may dry up completely in shallow marshes during dry periods.

Pileated Woodpecker

Wood Duck

Swamp

Where would you be if you were walking through a forest and wading through water at the same time? If you said a swamp, you're right. Swamps are woods with water-filled soils that are flooded in the spring by nearby streams or rivers. The flooding is caused by the water from melting snow. Woody-stemmed shrubs and trees grow well in the wet soils. By the end of the summer, you may not be able to see the water in a swamp anymore, but just take a walk through the trees and your squishy, mucky sneakers will soon show you that the water isn't very far away. Swamps are home to lots of wildlife all year long. They are especially important habitats, or homes, in the winter when woodpeckers come to tap the trees for bugs, and deer and Snowshoe Hares take shelter from the wind as they nibble on the tender buds of the shrubs and young trees.

Bog

If you think the ground only shakes during an earthquake, then you should visit a bog. If you bounce on a quaking bog, you'll feel the ground move, or quake. That's because the ground in a bog isn't solid earth like your backyard; it's made of peat. Peat is the dead remains of plants, mostly mosses, that have piled up in deep layers over many years. Peat is full of holes that soak up water like a sponge, making the ground squishy and wet.

Bogs are most common in northern climates where evergreen trees and shrubs can grow above the bog's thick carpet of sphagnum moss. Many bogs have formed in deep, bowl-like depressions that were left by glaciers during the last ice age, thousands of years ago. Like a bowl, there are no drainage holes to let water escape, so bogs are filled with water that's been sitting there a long time. This stagnant water has very little oxygen but lots of acid from the decaying moss. Moss can grow from the edge of the water, out over the water, to form a floating mat of moss. As the mosses die, they drop to the bottom of the bowl and may eventually fill up the entire depression. Never walk on floating mats of moss; you could easily fall through into the water below. Even solid peat should be avoided because bogs can be easily damaged by people walking on them. Boardwalks are built in parks and nature reserves to help preserve the delicate bog and to let people get a closer look at the many interesting plants that grow there.

Because the water in a bog is acidic and has little oxygen, very few animals live there. Without the tiny animals that help plants rot, such as bacteria, dead plants may lie in a bog for thousands of years without decaying and turning back into soil. Scientists use bogs as nature's time capsules to search for clues of the past. Pollen from trees that grew 10 000 years ago has been found in bogs, helping researchers discover what kinds of plants grew there long ago. Almost anything that falls into a bog can be well preserved, even people. In 1950, Danish workers uncovered a nearly perfectly preserved body of a man who had died 2000 years ago — and he still needed a shave!

Bog checklist
- most common in northern areas
- carpeted with sphagnum moss
- evergreen trees and shrubs
- layers of peat
- stagnant, acidic water with no drainage

Pitcher plant

Sphagnum moss

Fen

Like a bog, a fen is a northern wetland that is also formed on peat. While a bog is like a plugged up sink with no drainage, a fen is more like a bucket with a slow leak. Water flows very slowly in a fen, but it's enough to rinse out the acid water created by the peat and mosses. Because fens aren't acidic, they are home to many kinds of plants that can't survive in bogs, such as sedges, grasses, willows, Dwarf Birches and even cattails.

Fen checklist
- most common in northern areas
- lots of sedges, grasses and low shrubs
- layers of peat
- very slow-moving water
- not acidic

Grass or sedge?

Can you tell the difference between grasses and sedges? Here's an easy way to do it. Hold a stem between your thumb and forefinger and roll it around. You'll find that grass has a smooth, round stem and a sedge has a three-sided stem that doesn't roll smoothly in your fingers. To remember the difference, just think of the simple rhyme, "sedges have edges." You'll find lots of sedges in a fen.

Wetland Summary

TYPE OF WETLAND	Marsh	Swamp	Bog	Fen
	Cattail	Blueberry 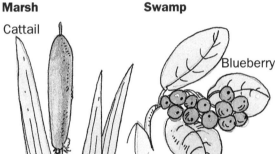	Sphagnum Moss	Pitcher-plant
Location	• along shores of rivers, streams and coasts, in shallows of ponds and lakes, or in potholes	• along rivers, streams and lakes	• in northern climates • often in deep depressions with no drainage	• in northern climates • usually in low-lying areas with some drainage
Plant life	• soft-stemmed emergents such as cattail and arrowhead	• mainly woody-stemmed plants such as shrubs and trees	• layers of peat • evergreen trees and shrubs • a surface carpet of sphagnum moss • insect-eating plants	• layers of peat • sedges, grasses and low shrubs • insect-eating plants
Water	• up to 2 m (7 feet) of water • small marshes may dry up in the summer	• shallow water that may dry up by the end of the summer	• stagnant and acidic water, sometimes covered with a floating mat of moss • open water may be very deep	• slow-moving, shallow surface water that may dry up during summer

Wetland wardrobe

Now that you know what a wetland is, you're ready to get your feet wet. Turn the page for your first wetland adventure, but first grab your gear, get your wetland wardrobe together and read the tips on the next page.

Hat to keep off insects and sun

Backpack

Long-sleeved shirt to avoid insect bites and scratches from plants

Long pants tucked into boots for walking through tall plants

Tall rubber boots

What to bring

- ☐ lunch or snacks and water
- ☐ insect repellent
- ☐ binoculars (wetlands are great places for birdwatching)
- ☐ plastic magnifying glass for getting a close look at plants and tiny animals such as insects and snails
- ☐ field guides to pond life, insects, fish, wildflowers, trees or birds
- ☐ pad and pencil for making notes or sketches
- ☐ camera

Safety tips

- [ ] take a friend or an adult along when you visit wetlands
- [ ] avoid steep banks and slippery shoreline rocks
- [ ] use gently sloping shores to get access to the water
- [ ] never walk on a frozen marsh or pond

Wetland conservation tips

Exploring a wetland is a lot of fun, but remember that you're visiting the home of many plants and animals. Here are a few ways that you can help keep their habitat safe.

- [ ] stay on the trails and boardwalks so you don't crush the wetland plants
- [ ] enjoy the wildflowers where they are instead of picking them
- [ ] be careful not to disturb or frighten wildlife. The quieter you are, the better your chance of seeing wetland animals.
- [ ] always take your garbage out of the wetland. If you carry a plastic bag in your pack, you can also pick up litter left by others and make the wetland a better place for everyone.
- [ ] set up your aquarium at home before bringing any plants or animals home for temporary observation. Always return the plants and animals to where you found them in the wetland.

15

Exploring mud

If you like splashing through mud and looking for buried treasure, then you're ready for a wetland adventure. Head down to the marshy part of a nearby pond or stream and sink your feet (and fingers) into some marvellous mud. You'll be amazed at what you'll find.

You'll need:
- a pail
- a light-coloured, shallow plastic container such as a dishpan
- water from a wetland
- a kitchen strainer (tied to a broom handle for a longer reach)
- tweezers or a tiny paintbrush
- a magnifying glass

1. Fill your pail and shallow container with clear water from the wetland.

2. Choose a spot on the edge of the marsh where you can safely stand and dip your strainer into the water. Carefully scoop up some mud from the bottom with your strainer.

3. To uncover the creatures hiding in the mud, bob your strainer up and down in the pail of water, making sure the water never goes over the lip of the strainer. The mud will be washed away and you'll be left with tiny animals, bits of decaying plants, or other things too big to fit through the strainer's holes.

4. Using tweezers or a damp paint brush, transfer any animals that you find in your strainer into the shallow container. The light-coloured bottom of the pan will make the animals easy to see. Use the magnifying glass to get a closer look at the creatures. Look at their different shapes, sizes and colours, and discover how the animals move around. Keep the container out of the sun.

5. Try scooping up mud in different areas of the marsh: along the shore, in shallow water and in deep water. Compare the numbers and different kinds of animals that you find.

6. When you have finished looking at the animals, return everything to the marsh.

Life in the mud

Look for these animals in the marsh mud:

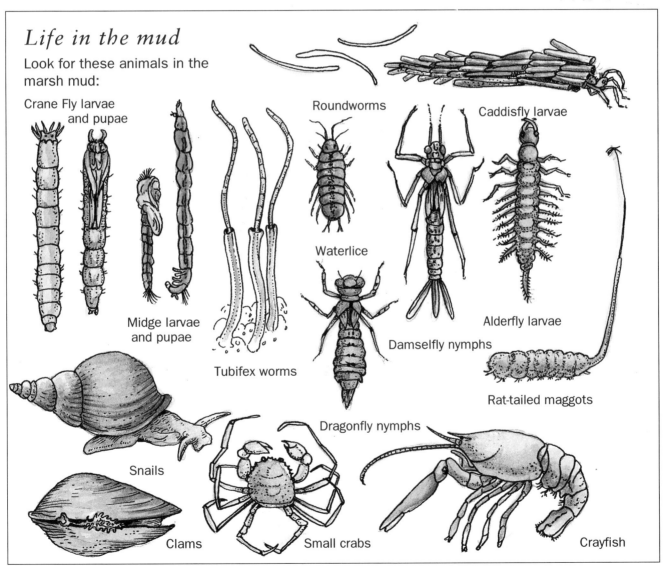

Crane Fly larvae and pupae

Roundworms

Caddisfly larvae

Midge larvae and pupae

Waterlice

Tubifex worms

Damselfly nymphs

Alderfly larvae

Rat-tailed maggots

Dragonfly nymphs

Snails

Clams

Small crabs

Crayfish

Peeking at peat

After you put leaves into your compost pile, they slowly break down into a terrific soil mixture full of nutrients. If you put the same kind of leaves into a bog, they may still be there 10 000 years from now without much change. A bog is a bit like a giant pickle jar. The plant and animal materials that fall into a bog don't rot; they stay fresh for years. Like pickle juice, bog water is acidic, and this helps to preserve things. Most bacteria, fungi and other tiny creatures that help plants rot can't live in boggy water because it is too acidic and hasn't much oxygen. So as more materials are added to the bog, the layers just get deeper and deeper instead of breaking down. The organic matter (something that was alive) on the bottom of the bog gets squished under the weight of the new layers. Eventually the flattened materials form peat. You've probably heard of peat moss. Companies dig peat out of wetlands, dry it, call it peat moss and sell it in garden centres.

Moss-covered bog

TRY THIS! *Poke into peat*

If you wanted to find out what your neighbourhood looked like before you were born, you could ask people who have lived there for a long time, or you could look at old photographs. But finding out what the neighbourhood looked like 10 000 years ago is a bit more difficult. One way scientists find out what Earth looked like before people lived here is to visit bogs. They drill small holes deep into a bog and pull out tubes of peat, called core samples. The sections of a core sample come from different layers of peat and were formed at different times. By dissecting, or taking apart, the sample, researchers find bits of plants and animal parts. When these bits and pieces are identified, the scientists discover what plants and animals lived in the area long ago. They can even tell how long the plants and animals have been in the bog. You can dissect some peat yourself and discover some of the plants or animals that helped to make it.

You'll need:
- a small shovel or trowel
- peat
- a shallow dishpan
- a magnifying glass
- a field guide to trees (optional)

1. Visit a bog where you can safely reach some open ground, preferably from a boardwalk. Dig a narrow hole as far down as you can reach. Be careful not to disturb the surrounding area.

2. With the edge of your shovel, cut a slice of peat about 1 cm (1/2 inch) thick from the side of your hole. Try to slice from the surface all the way to the bottom of the hole at one go.

3. Carefully pull your slice out of the hole, holding it against the shovel so the slice stays in one piece.

4. Lay the slice of peat in the bottom of your dishpan. Can you see different layers between the bottom and top of the slice? Separate the peat with your fingers and look for seeds and bits of leaves, branches or roots.

5. Use the magnifying glass to find tiny pieces. If you find large pieces of leaves, you can use a field guide to try to identify them. Are the plant parts at the bottom of the slice the same as those near the top? You should find that the materials that came from the surface are less decomposed than those you found farther down.

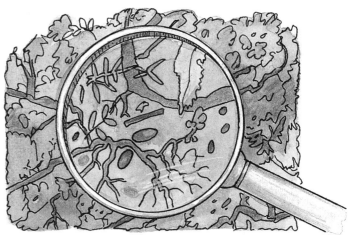

6. When you have finished looking at the peat, carefully return it and fill in the hole.

Nature's sponges

Sphagnum moss

What do mosses and diapers have in common? Both absorb wetness. Long ago, North American Natives actually used layers of moss inside their babies' pants for the same reason we use diapers today. Sphagnum mosses, which grow in bogs, can absorb so much water that they act like super sponges. This comes in handy when flooding starts because the bog can soak up some of the extra water and reduce flooding problems.

Other wetlands found along streams and rivers also help reduce flooding. They act as large, shallow basins where flood waters can collect and spread out. The level and speed of water in the stream or river goes down as the flood water spreads through the wetlands. This helps keep the flood under control. There is often much less flood damage to towns near wetlands than to towns where there are no wetlands or where wetlands have been destroyed.

Wetlands also keep you from getting thirsty. Water held in a wetland can slowly sink into the ground. This helps refill the system of underground streams and pools that fill the wells that supply drinking water to many small towns.

EXPERIMENT! *A water race*

Find out which kind of soil is the best sponge for holding water by having a water race. In this race the slowest competitor wins!

You'll need:
- 3 1-L (4-cup) plastic pop bottles
- scissors or a sharp knife
- tape
- cheesecloth or a J-cloth
- 3 elastic bands
- 3 clear, wide-mouthed jars
- dry sand
- dry garden soil
- dry sphagnum moss or peat moss (from a garden centre)
- a measuring cup
- water
- a watch with a second hand
- a pencil and notebook

1. Ask an adult to cut the pop bottles in half across the middle. You will use the top half, with the spout. Tape over the sharp edges so you don't cut yourself.

2. Place a piece of cheesecloth over the spout of each pop bottle and secure it with an elastic band.

3. Turn each bottle upside-down and sit it in the mouth of a jar. Fill half of each bottle with a different kind of soil.

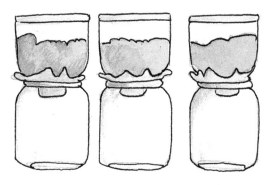

4. Slowly pour 250 mL (1 cup) of water into one of the bottles. Use a watch to time how long it takes the water to start filtering through the soil into the jar below. Then time how long the water continues to drip through. Record your results in a notebook and then test the other soil types.

5. Use the measuring cup to measure the amount of water in each jar. Which soil absorbed the most water? The soil that drained the least is the best soil for holding water. To figure out how much water each soil type absorbed, use this formula:

$$250 \text{ mL (1 cup)} - \begin{array}{c} \text{amount of} \\ \text{water in jar} \end{array} = \begin{array}{c} \text{amount of water} \\ \text{absorbed by soil} \end{array}$$

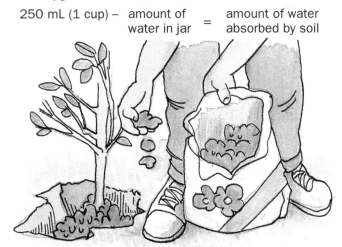

What's happening?

Water needs open areas to flow through, so the soil with the most air spaces allowed the water to drain the fastest. The large, loosely packed particles of sand have lots of air space between them and let the water run through quickly. The garden soil has smaller particles that are more tightly packed and have less space between them, so the water moved more slowly. Pure peat moss has very fine particles and trapped the water the best. Damp peat moss is often used in garden centres as packing around plants to keep them moist. You can add peat moss to the soil in your garden to help hold the water in the soil longer and conserve water.

What happens if ...

... you mix peat moss with the sand or the garden soil and then repeat the experiment? How does the peat affect their ability to hold water?

Filtering the flow

Have you ever noticed that rivers sometimes look brown after a big storm? Heavy rains wash soil and other materials, together called sediment, into the river. The sediment gets carried along in the water, making the river brown. Too much sediment in a river clogs the gills of fish and other aquatic life. It also covers their eggs so that no oxygen can get to them and the babies suffocate. Sediment may contain fertilizers or harmful chemicals that cause pollution in a river. These extra ingredients cause too much algae to grow — when it decays, the oxygen in the water is used up.

Wetlands help make river water clean again. Wetland plants act like filters. They let the water through but trap the sediment the way a sieve traps spaghetti and allows the water to run down the drain. Wetland plants such as cattails and Pickerelweed trap fertilizers, using them to grow, and can also absorb many harmful chemicals. By trapping and absorbing sediment, wetland plants keep it from creating pollution problems downstream.

EXPERIMENT!

Set a sediment trap

Plant a sediment trap in a box to see how a wetland helps filter flowing water in streams and rivers.

You'll need:
- 2 small boxes the same size (shoe boxes work well)
- plastic bags
- garden soil
- a piece of sod (from a garden centre or your lawn)
- scissors
- a straw
- some books or blocks of wood
- 2 pails
- 2 cups
- a measuring cup
- water
- a tea bag
- a small spoon or wire whisk

1. Line the inside of each of the boxes with plastic bags to make them waterproof.

2. In one box, place 5 cm (2 inches) of garden soil over the bottom of the box. Cover half of the soil with a thick piece of sod (soil with grass growing in it) and pack soil onto the other half until it is level with the base of the grass. The grass represents the wetland plants.

3. Fill the second box with garden soil to the same depth as the soil in the first box.

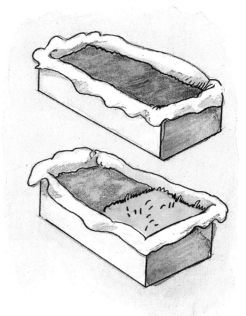

4. With the point of the scissors, make a small hole to fit the straw in the end of each box, just above the soil line. In the first box, the hole should be placed at the sod end.

5. Cut a straw in half and poke each half part way into each of the holes so that it pierces the plastic liner in the box. The straw will be your drain spout.

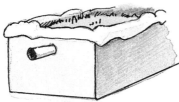

6. Set your two boxes side by side at the edge of a table or counter, with the straw sticking out over the edge. Place a couple of books or pieces of wood under the back end of each box so that each box is sloping the same amount. The slope will make the water move quickly, as it does in a fast river or stream.

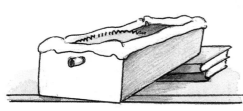

7. Place a pail on the floor under each straw to catch the water when it flows out.

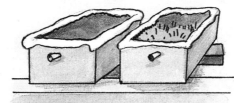

8. Put 250 mL (1 cup) of water in each cup. Cut open a tea bag and sprinkle half of the tea into each cup. The tea leaves represent the sediment in the water. Stir up the water so the tea leaves are floating around.

9. Quickly pour one cup into the soil at the back of each box. Watch what happens to the water as it flows through the box and drains out the other end.

10. Check the water in each pail. Which pail contains the most tea leaves? What else is in the pails?

What's happening?
The moving water picked up soil particles as it flowed through the box of soil. Because the water slowed down as it entered the narrow straw, some of its load settled, staying in the box, but much of it washed out into the pail, like river water carrying its sediment downstream. You should have found that the water that flowed through the box of soil carried most of its tea leaves, as well as some soil, into the bucket. The water that flowed through the sod was slowed down by the roots and stems of the plants, which trapped most of the sediment (soil and tea), filtering it out of the water. When the water flowed downstream (to the pail), it was much cleaner.

Saving shorelines

Have you ever built a sandcastle too close to the water at the beach? When a big wave rolls in, the water washes over the sandcastle and carries it away. The same thing happens to the soil along the shores of rivers, streams, lakes and oceans. When waves hit the shore or heavy rain pours down, some of the soil is washed away. Sometimes powerful waves during a storm can break off whole chunks of land. This washing away of earth is called erosion. Wetland plants along shorelines help stop erosion. The roots of the plants grow through the soil and knit together, holding the soil in place. The stems and leaves of the plants also protect shorelines. Some people who live along coasts or lakeshores where wetland plants have been destroyed have lost their land or homes because of erosion.

A pot of roots

Plant a mini radish-patch in a pot and discover how the radish roots hold onto the soil even after the pot is removed.

You'll need:
- radish seeds
- a saucer
- water
- potting soil
- a 10-cm (4-inch) flowerpot with drainage holes

1. Place about 12 radish seeds in a saucer and cover them with shallow water. Leave the seeds to soak for a day or so until tiny sprouts appear.

2. Put soil in a flowerpot, three-quarters of the way to the top. Place the sprouted seeds in the pot and cover them with a thin layer of soil. Water the soil until it is damp and put the pot in a sunny window. Keep the soil damp.

3. Three weeks after the radish seedlings appear, your radish plants should be growing well. Hold onto the plants with one hand and gently remove the flowerpot with the other.

What's happening?
When you take the flowerpot away, you should find that most of the soil remains in the shape of the pot. The white, thread-like lines woven through the soil are radish roots, which are holding the soil together. All plant roots help trap soil and keep it from being washed away. Carefully separate your radish seedlings and plant them outside in your garden so you can enjoy a tasty treat in a few weeks.

Investigating Wetlands

There's more to wetlands than meets the eye. Just experiment with some marsh water at home and you'll soon discover the plankton that live in it, often unseen. Larger wetland animals may also be hard to see at first because of their excellent camouflage. In this section you'll learn how to discover and identify the tracks of unseen wetland animals. Go on a night prowl to spy on the nightlife in a wetland. Even in winter, wetlands are full of interesting and active wildlife. So read on, then grab a friend and start investigating wetlands for yourself.

Grow some plankton

You can see many different types of plants in a marsh, but some of the most important ones are so small you need a magnifying glass or microscope to see them. These are the phytoplankton, tiny green plants that float around in water. Phytoplankton (also called algae) are eaten by zooplankton (tiny floating animals) and insects, which are eaten by small fish. The small fish are eaten by large fish, which in turn are eaten by birds and mammals, including people. You can catch some plankton to watch it grow and get a close look at these amazing tiny plants.

You'll need:
- a large plastic container with a lid (a big ice-cream tub works well)
- marsh water
- a large glass jar
- a magnifying glass
- a microscope, glass slide and eye dropper (optional)

1. Carefully scoop some clear water out of a marsh with your plastic container. Try not to get any of the bottom muck or large plants in the tub. Put on the lid and take the water home.

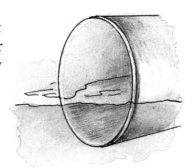

2. At home, transfer the water to a clean jar with no lid and put the jar in a bright window.

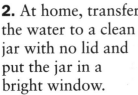

3. After a few days, you will notice the water starting to turn green; it may also be a bit cloudy. The green colour comes from the phytoplankton, or algae, that is growing in the water. As the algae multiply, the water will become greener and cloudier.

4. Look at the water with your magnifying glass. Can you see some tiny clumps of algae? If you have a microscope, use an eye dropper to place a drop of marsh water on a glass slide. Look through the microscope to see the variety of plankton in the water. In general, the green-coloured organisms are phytoplankton and the fast-moving, clear organisms are zooplankton.

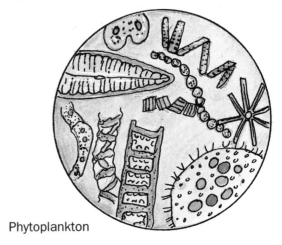

Phytoplankton

5. When you've finished looking at your plankton, return the marsh water to the wetland.

What happens if ...

... you cover your jar with black paper so that no light reaches the water for a few days? What happens to the colour of the water?

... you put your jar in the fridge? How does the cold affect the growth of your plankton?

EXPERIMENT!

Where's the leaf?

Zooplankton are important recyclers in wetlands, helping to break down the dead and decaying plants that fall into the water. Here's an underwater experiment that you can do with the help of these invisible animals to find out how hard they work.

You'll need:
- a large plastic container with a lid (a big ice-cream tub works well)
- marsh water
- a dead leaf from a marsh plant
- a large glass jar
- a pencil
- thread
- tape

1. Fill a plastic container with clear water from a marsh. Bring the water home, along with a dead leaf from a marsh plant. Pour the water into the glass jar.

2. Place the jar in a bright window for a day. Lay a pencil across the opening of the jar. Tie one end of a piece of thread to the leaf stem and the other end to the pencil so that the leaf is suspended in the water. The leaf may float at first, but it will eventually sink. Secure the pencil in place with tape.

3. Leave the jar in the sun for a week and watch what happens. The tiny zooplankton in the marsh water will feed on the leaf until eventually there will be nothing left but a leaf skeleton.

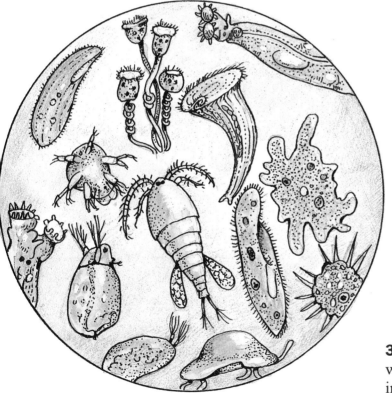

Zooplankton

29

Camouflage in a wetland

Hide-and-seek is a fun game, but for wetland wildlife it's a matter of life and death. Animals that can hide from their enemies live longer than those that can't. And animals that can sneak up on their prey without being seen catch the most food. When an animal's colour or shape helps it blend in with the environment, it's called camouflage. Many wetland animals have excellent camouflage to help them hide in the reeds and water. Can you find the 10 animals hiding in the marsh on these pages? Turn to page 96 for the answers.

Tracking wetland wildlife

TRY THIS!

Have you ever forgotten to take off your dirty shoes and left a trail of muddy footprints to your room? Wildlife often leave their prints or tracks in the mud around wetlands, too. Finding animal tracks is a great way to discover what wildlife use a wetland. You can collect animal tracks by making plaster casts of the tracks. Gather the materials below and get tracking.

You'll need:

- several cardboard strips 3 cm (1 inch) wide and 40–50 cm (15–20 inches) long
- stapler or tape
- about 1 kg (2 pounds) of plain Plaster of Paris or other plaster mix (from a hardware or craft-supply store)
- two plastic containers with lids (yoghurt or margarine containers work well)
- salt
- water
- a small stick for stirring
- paper and pencil
- a field guide to animal tracks (optional)
- wire (optional)
- newspaper
- an old toothbrush
- fine sandpaper

1. Visit the damp, muddy shore of a marsh. Look for a well-formed, deep track that has not been disturbed. Make a cardboard ring out of one of the strips to put around the track, allowing 3 cm (1 inch) of space on all sides. Staple or tape the two edges of cardboard together. Press the ring firmly into the mud.

2. Mix up the plaster in one of your containers according to the directions on the package. Add a pinch of salt to the dry plaster before adding water, to make it harden faster. Always add plaster to the water (instead of water to the plaster) to make the mixing easier. Stir the plaster mixture with your stick until it is smooth and has the consistency of porridge. If it is too thin, add more plaster.

3. Tap the bottom of your container sharply on the ground a few times to get any air bubbles in the plaster to rise to the surface. Air bubbles make holes in the plaster that can cause your cast to break.

4. Carefully pour the plaster mixture into the track until it almost fills the cardboard ring. Leave about .5 cm (1/4 inch) of space at the top.

5. Smooth the surface of the plaster with your stick or finger, and let it set for 20–30 minutes. Make a note of where your track is (kind of habitat, such as marsh or bog, and location) as well as the date. If you have a field guide, try to identify what animal made the track.

6. When the cast is semi-hard, you may want to set a small wire loop into the back. This can be used for hanging the cast up for display.

7. Once the plaster is hard, remove the cardboard ring and lift the cast up. Wrap it in newspaper to take it home. If some mud sticks to the plaster, let the mud dry and then brush it off with your fingers or an old toothbrush. Rough edges can be lightly sanded with fine sandpaper.

Winter tracks

You can make animal tracking a year-round hobby. With a simple trick of the trade, you can make plaster casts of winter tracks to add to your collection. In addition to the materials listed under "Tracking wetland wildlife," you'll need a water sprayer, sometimes used for spraying houseplants or for cleaning windows.

The best casts of winter tracks are made on very cold days in hard-packed snow. When you find a good track, lightly spray a film of cold water in the track and let it freeze. This coats the track with a thin, smooth layer of ice that makes a good surface for the plaster to harden on. Then make your cast the same way as before. Since the plaster takes longer to dry in the winter, you'll have time to look for more tracks or other animal clues while you wait.

Look for these animal tracks around wetlands:

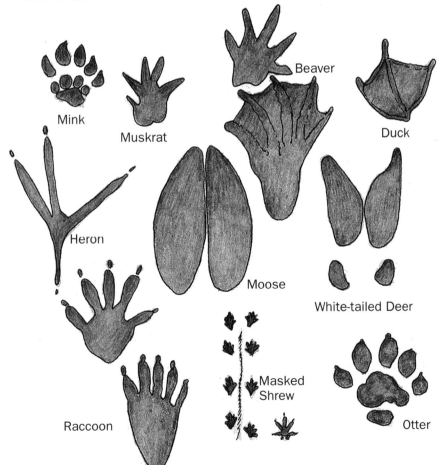

Mink

Muskrat

Beaver

Duck

Heron

Moose

White-tailed Deer

Raccoon

Masked Shrew

Otter

Wetlands in winter

Imagine having a roof made of ice. In winter the ice that covers marshes and ponds makes a roof for the watery world of the creatures that live there all winter long. You can discover some winter wildlife by taking a hike to a marsh. Dress warmly, pack a hot Thermos for you and a friend and head out to discover what is going on in a winter wetland. Remember: Never walk out on the ice and avoid the thin ice near shorelines and around rocks and stumps.

Aquatic mammals in winter

You'd freeze if you took a dip in winter wetland water, but mink, otter, beaver and muskrat are all well adapted to surviving under the ice. They travel beneath it in search of food. Their thick layers of fat and dense fur provide terrific insulation against the cold. Their fur is also waterproofed by oils from special glands, so the animals never really feel wet.

You may see some of these animals, or clues they've left behind, on your hike. Look for mink tracks in the snow along the shore. The otter is a large cousin to the mink, and it is famous for its otter slides. Playful otters will climb a snowbank by a frozen lake and slide down on their bellies with their legs stretched out. Watch for signs of otter slides along the banks.

A beaver's food and the entrance to its home are both underwater, so it rarely surfaces in the winter. But you may find a beaver lodge of mud and sticks with steam rising from it. The steam comes from the warm breath of the beavers inside. Muskrats also prefer to stay under the ice to feed on plants, crayfish, freshwater clams and mussels, but sometimes their shallow-water homes freeze solid to the bottom. When this happens, the muskrats have to travel over the snow to eat dry grasses, weeds and willow twigs on land.

Otter

Sound sleepers

Although you won't hear them snoring, some animals are sound asleep under the ice, buried in the muddy marsh sediment. Frogs and turtles are cold-blooded. This means that their body temperature is controlled by the outside temperature. When the weather gets too cold, their bodies can't work properly, so cold-blooded animals hibernate and sleep until spring arrives. Fish are also cold-blooded, but some fish do well in cold water and stay active all winter. Yellow Perch and Northern Pike, for instance, spend the winter quite happily in deep water, which is warmer than the water at the icy surface. As spring approaches, the surface water warms up and the fish move to the shallows. Other species, such as sunfish, bass and catfish, bury themselves in the muddy bottom or under dead leaves in shallow water near the shore.

Yellow Perch

Icy insects

You won't get any mosquito bites in a wintry marsh, but you may see other insects. Water Boatmen and backswimmers huddle together in air pockets under the ice or cling to the remains of plants. During a thaw you may see water striders at the surface or Diving Beetles swimming around.

Diving Beetles

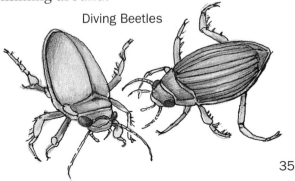

Nature's nurseries

Marshes are sometimes called nature's nurseries because so many animals are born there. If you visit a marsh in late spring or early summer, you may discover some of the eggs that marsh mothers have laid and left. Take a close look at the shoreline plants and shallow waters to discover several different marsh species that begin their lives as eggs. Check out the scene on these pages so you'll know what to look for.

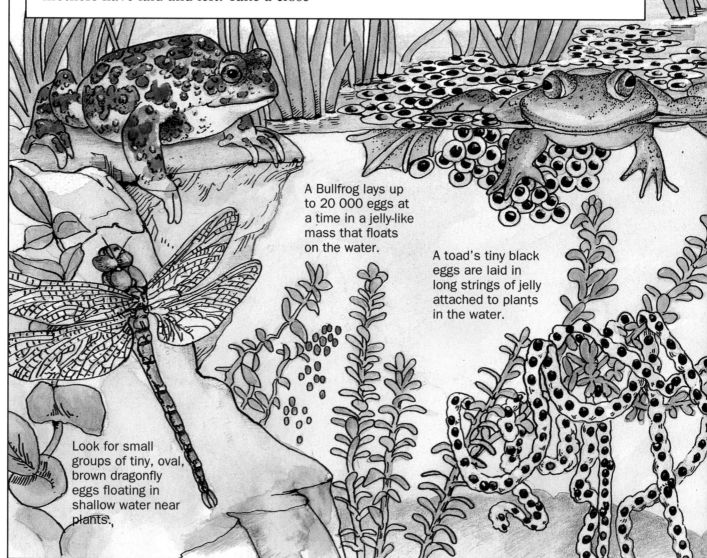

A Bullfrog lays up to 20 000 eggs at a time in a jelly-like mass that floats on the water.

A toad's tiny black eggs are laid in long strings of jelly attached to plants in the water.

Look for small groups of tiny, oval, brown dragonfly eggs floating in shallow water near plants.

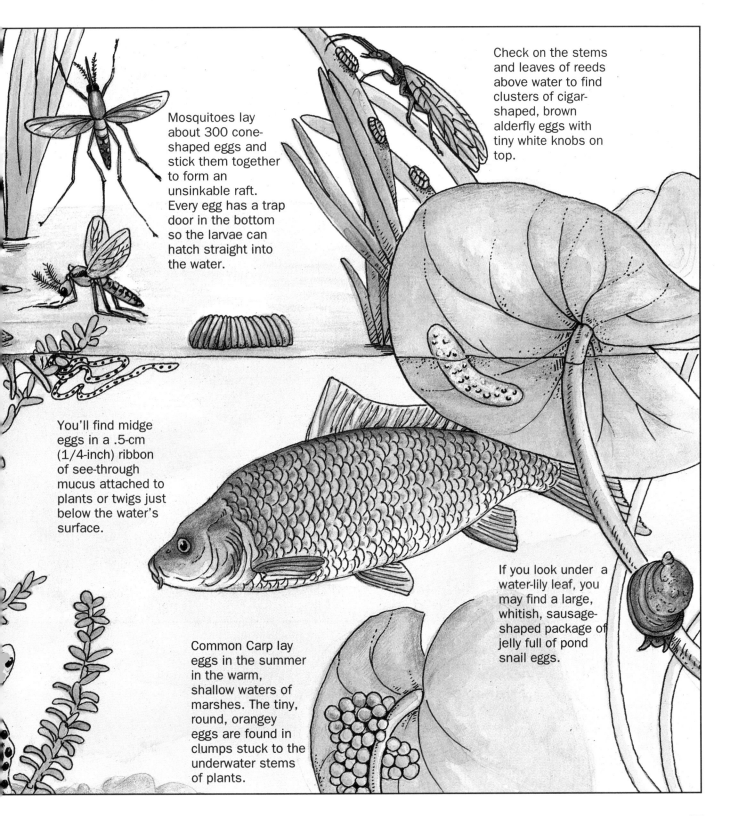

Mosquitoes lay about 300 cone-shaped eggs and stick them together to form an unsinkable raft. Every egg has a trap door in the bottom so the larvae can hatch straight into the water.

Check on the stems and leaves of reeds above water to find clusters of cigar-shaped, brown alderfly eggs with tiny white knobs on top.

You'll find midge eggs in a .5-cm (1/4-inch) ribbon of see-through mucus attached to plants or twigs just below the water's surface.

If you look under a water-lily leaf, you may find a large, whitish, sausage-shaped package of jelly full of pond snail eggs.

Common Carp lay eggs in the summer in the warm, shallow waters of marshes. The tiny, round, orangey eggs are found in clumps stuck to the underwater stems of plants.

Wetlands at night

Wetlands are terrific wildlife habitats, providing food, shelter and protection to many animals. Wildlife from other habitats, such as fields and forests, also use wetlands, even though they don't make their homes there. These wildlife visitors often come to wetlands at night where they can hide from predators or sneak up on prey. Water is the main attraction for many animals. Deer, moose and fox will often head to the marsh at dusk for a drink. Skunks and raccoons visit the water's edge for a delicious meal of duck or turtle eggs. Toads, treefrogs and salamanders come to the marsh to mate and lay eggs on warm spring nights. When the eggs hatch, the young live in the water. They move to the land when they turn into adults. The night sky is full of activity, too. Overhead, a silent shadow passes by — an owl in search of a four-legged feast, such as a mouse or shrew. Acrobatic bats perform swoops and dives, as they capture hundreds of night-flying insects.

You can be a night visitor to a wetland, too. Find a flashlight and an adult, and head to a marsh or swamp at dusk. If you have a tape recorder, bring it along. The nighttime noises are amazing, and you'll have fun listening to the tape the next day and trying to guess what makes each of the different sounds. Although you can't see in the dark as well as an owl can, you may still catch sight of a pair of bright, shining eyes in the night, especially if you use your flashlight. Some night prowlers, such as raccoons, have special cells in their eyes that work like mirrors. By reflecting light that comes into the eyes, these cells make more light. This helps raccoons see well in the dark. The brightness you see in their eyes is called eye shine.

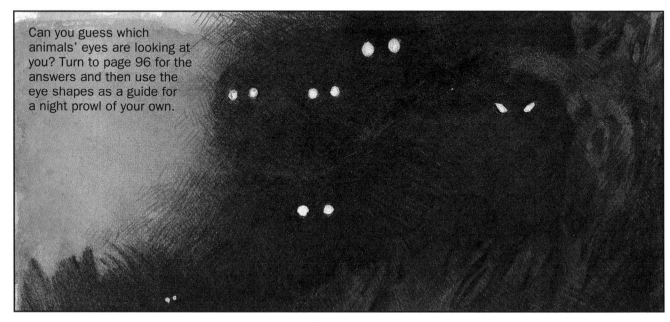

Can you guess which animals' eyes are looking at you? Turn to page 96 for the answers and then use the eye shapes as a guide for a night prowl of your own.

Night prowl

You'll need:
- black construction paper
- scissors
- fluorescent paint and a paintbrush, or reflective tape (from a hardware or craft-supply store)
- black thumbtacks
- a flashlight

1. Cut out several small squares of black paper. On each paper, paint a pair of eyes to look like the eyes of a nighttime wetland animal. If you use reflective tape, stick it onto the paper then cut out the eye shapes.

2. During the afternoon, close to home, tack your eye pictures to tree trunks, logs, bushes and buildings at heights suitable to each animal. For instance, an owl's eyes would be as high up in a tree as you can reach, while a skunk's eyes would be closer to the ground.

3. When it's dark, have your friends walk around with flashlights to try to find the shining eyes. Who can find the most eyes and who can guess what animals they belong to?

4. Remember to collect your papers and thumbtacks the next day so they don't become litter.

Discovering Wetland Wildlife

Wetlands are one of the best places to enjoy nature. Listen to a chorus of frogs and toads, peek at some underwater plants, scan the rocks for sunbathing reptiles or catch some tiny water insects. There's always a new discovery to make in a wetland. Read on to find out how to set up a mini-wetland at home in an aquarium so you can get a closer look at some wetland creatures.

Mapping a bird's breeding territory

If you didn't want people wandering through your property, you might put up "no trespassing" signs. Birds simply sing to get rid of unwanted visitors. One of the loudest singers in the marsh is the male Red-winged Blackbird. Its tropical-sounding "ok-a-ree" song is a warning to everyone to go away. The male, which has red wing patches, is defending its nesting territory. Nearby, its mate is tending to a nest of eggs or young. The female is brown, like the plant stems she's hiding in, so you'll find it hard to spot her.

Birds usually sing from high perches, where their voices will carry farther through the air. Watch where the Red-winged Blackbirds perch. You'll see them on the tops of cattail heads, high shrubs or nearby trees. By following the perching, flying, and singing patterns of a male Red-winged Blackbird, you can figure out where its territory lies within the marsh.

You'll need:
- paper
- a pencil with an eraser
- a clipboard
- binoculars

Red-winged Blackbird

1. Choose an area where Red-winged Blackbirds are active. Find a high spot to stand, close to the edge of a marsh, where you have a wide view across the cattails. An ideal spot is the observation deck of a marsh boardwalk.

2. Draw a map-like picture of the marsh before you. Use clumps of shoreline shrubs, bright flowers, a muskrat mound, a boardwalk, etc., as landmarks on your picture. Draw the features so that the distance between landmarks on your picture is relative to the same distances in the marsh.

3. Choose one male Red-winged Blackbird and focus your binoculars on him. Make a mark on your map to indicate where he is sitting. Follow the bird for several minutes as it flies, perches and sings in different spots in the marsh. Whenever the bird sets down, make another mark on your map at that location. When the male returns to its original perch, or nearby, look at your map. Join all the marks together with lines to show the whole territory.

What's happening?

The marks you have made on the map indicate the boundaries of the bird's territory. How large is the territory of your Red-winged Blackbird? The size of a bird's territory depends partly on how much food there is in the marsh, the availability of good nesting sites, and the size of the local population of Red-winged Blackbirds. If the food supply and nesting sites are plentiful, more birds can live in a smaller area.

What happens if …

… you try the same activity with a different male Red-winged Blackbird? Does it fly into the territory of the first bird? Does it perch there?

Aquatic animals

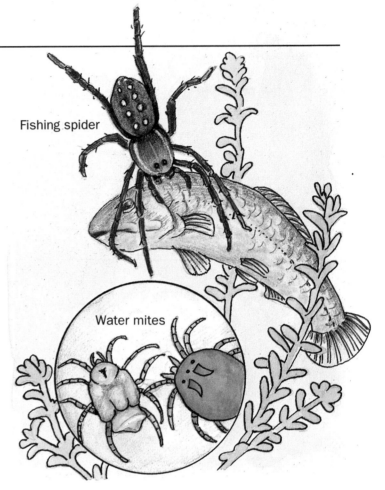

Fishing spider

Water mites

If you take a close look at the water in a marsh, you'll find a great assortment of aquatic insects, spiders, mites and other small animals. These animals provide food for fish, frogs, turtles and other wetland wildlife. Some of the small creatures are predators themselves. The fishing spider dangles the tip of one leg in the water to attract tiny fish. When a fish swims within reach, the spider lunges off its floating leaf to catch it. Once caught, the fish is bitten and poisoned by the spider and dragged back onto the leaf. The bright red bodies of water mites are easy to spot in the water. These tiny creatures also attack prey much larger than themselves, including small crustaceans, insect larvae and aquatic worms. The mites attach themselves to their prey and suck out the body juices with their tiny, straw-like mouths.

TRY THIS! *Stoop and scoop*

You can find spiders, mites and much more by stooping and scooping in the water at a marsh.

You'll need:
- rubber gloves (good in cold water)
- a shallow, light-coloured dishpan
- marsh water
- a kitchen strainer (tied to a broom handle for a longer reach)
- a tiny paintbrush
- a turkey baster
- small, clear plastic bottles (empty pill bottles work well)
- a magnifying glass
- field guides to pond life and insects

1. Find a gently sloping bank where you can safely reach the water. Fill the dishpan with clear marsh water and place it on the shore.

2. Look for any creatures swimming at the water's surface or clinging to floating leaves. Scoop them up with your strainer and gently transfer them to your dishpan with the paintbrush.

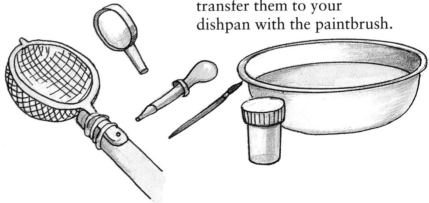

1. Water Boatman
2. Alderfly larva
3. Leech
4. Mosquito larva
5. Midge larva
6. Frog tadpole
7. Pond snail
8. Water Scorpion
9. Diving Beetle larva
10. Whirligig Beetle
11. Giant Water Bug

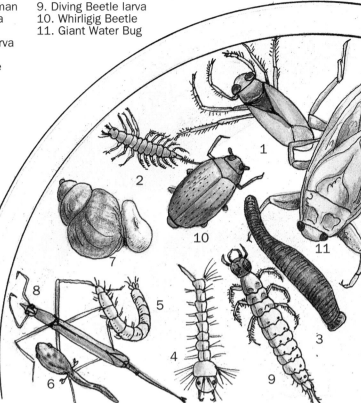

3. Dip your strainer underwater to catch any animals swimming deeper down. Add these to your dishpan, too.

4. For a closer look at something small, use the turkey baster to transfer an animal from your pan into a small bottle of marsh water. A magnifying glass will reveal the tiny creature's hairs, claws, mouthparts and other features that are hard to see with your eyes. Use a field guide to help you identify what you find.

5. When you have finished looking at the aquatic life, carefully return the animals and water to the marsh.

Night sight

Spy on underwater creatures at night with this simple trick. Turn on a bright flashlight and place it in a jar with a heavy stone. Seal the jar tightly so no water will get in. Tie a long string securely around the jar and lower the jar into shallow water while you hold on to the string. You'll be able to see anything that swims around the jar, and you may even attract the interest of some curious fish. Remember to take an adult along when you visit a wetland at night.

Peeking at plants

If you stay underwater for very long, you run out of oxygen and have to come up to the surface to take a breath. But how do the underwater roots of plants get air? You can see their amazing breathing system for yourself and compare it to the stem of a land-loving plant.

You'll need:
- a water-lily stem
- a sedge stem
- the stem of a daisy or other non-woody land plant (but not grass — it's hollow)
- scissors
- a magnifying glass
- a glass of water

1. Carefully cut each of the stems in half with scissors.

2. Take a close look at the cross sections of each stem with a magnifying glass. How do these cut ends compare?

3. Place one end of the water-lily stem into the glass of water so that it's under water. Put the other end in your mouth and blow out. Do you see bubbles in the water? Try this with the other stems too.

What's happening?

When you looked at the cut ends of the plant stems, you likely noticed that the aquatic plants had large air spaces, but the daisy stem was much denser, without large spaces. The stems of most aquatic plants are made of spongy tissue — they're full of holes. Air travels from the leaves above water, through the holy stems and down to the waterlogged roots. Notice the large size of the air spaces in the water-lily stems. Water-lilies have floating leaves attached to long, flexible underwater stems. The stems must have large air spaces to make them light and buoyant or their weight would drag the leaves under the water. Sedge stems have smaller air spaces. They need to be stiffer and stronger than water-lily stems to support their leaves and flowers in the air.

Cattails or bulrushes?

Can you tell the difference between a cattail and a bulrush? Many people think these wetlands plants are the same, but if you check out these pictures you'll see that they have many differences.

◄ Cattails (*Typha* species) are probably the easiest marsh plants to recognize. Their brown, cigar-shaped flower spikes contain over 10 000 tiny flowers and release thousands of white, fluffy seeds to the wind each fall. The hard, rounded stems and fluffy seed heads stand tall in the marsh all winter long and don't die down to the roots as do many other marsh plants. Red-winged Blackbirds use the old stalks to support their nests in early spring, long before other plants have grown.

Bulrushes (*Scirpus* species) are a type of sedge. Most bulrushes have solid, triangular stems, but a few, such as the hardstem bulrush, or tule, have round stems. The spear-like stems have small clusters of brown, scaly flowers hanging from their tips or, sometimes, along the stems. ►

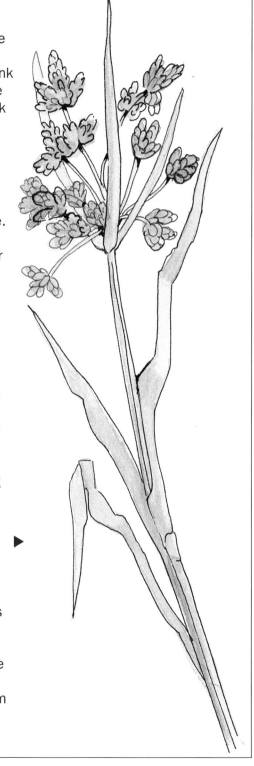

Grow some duckweed

Imagine a flower smaller than the head of a pin. Water meal, a kind of duckweed, is the smallest flowering plant in the world. You've probably seen duckweed floating like a green mat on the still water of a marsh or pond. A close look shows thousands of tiny floating plants with thread-like roots dangling in the water. Duckweed is one of the fastest spreading plants in a wetland. That's because, instead of only spreading by seeds as most plants do, these tiny green plants send out shoots that produce identical-looking plants complete with roots. The shoots break off from the parent plant and begin absorbing their own water and minerals from the marsh right away. These new plants make more new plants, until there is duckweed everywhere. Luckily for wetlands, waterbirds and insects eat their way through a lot of duckweed each year.

Because duckweed grows quickly, it is a good plant to use in experiments — you can get fast results that are easy to see. Collect some duckweed from a local marsh and try this simple experiment to find out what affect pollution may have on the growth of duckweed.

You'll need:
- a large plastic container (such as a large ice-cream tub)
- some duckweed
- clear marsh water
- a measuring cup
- 4 wide-mouthed plastic containers (yoghurt or margarine containers work well)
- tweezers
- lemon juice
- tomato juice
- apple juice
- labels (paper and tape will do)
- a spoon

1. Collect some duckweed and water from a marsh in a large plastic container.

2. Pour 250 mL (1 cup) of clear marsh water into a smaller plastic container and add 10 duckweed plants. Use tweezers to transfer them from the large container.

3. Pour 125 mL (1/2 cup) of one kind of juice into each of the other small containers and label them with the juice's name.

4. Add 125 mL (1/2 cup) of clear marsh water to each of these containers and stir the mixtures with a spoon. Lemon juice is 10 times more acidic than apple juice and over a hundred times more acidic than tomato juice. The juices represent acid pollution in a marsh.

5. Add 10 duckweed plants to each container of juice. Place all four containers in a sunny window.

6. Top up the water level with marsh water as necessary. After 10 days, count the number of duckweed plants in each container. How did the acids affect the growth of the duckweed?

7. When you are finished with your experiment, return the duckweed to the marsh and pour your juice mixtures down the drain.

What's happening?

You should find that the duckweed in the lemon juice grew the slowest because it is the most acidic. Pollution caused by driving automobiles and burning coal for electricity creates acids that can pollute waterways. Some plants and animals are very sensitive to rising acid levels, and thousands of lakes and waterways around the world have been seriously harmed by acid pollution.

What happens if …

… you add 5 mL (1 teaspoon) of baking soda to each container after you've observed the effects of the acids? Baking soda is alkaline (the opposite of acidic) and helps to reduce or reverse the effects of the acid pollution. Some marshes have limestone rock below their mud. Because limestone is alkaline, it helps protect these marshes from acid pollution.

… you grow duckweed in two containers of marsh water, placing one container in the fridge and leaving one at room temperature for a few weeks? The cold fridge represents the growing conditions of late fall. Which duckweed grows best?

Fun with fungi

Have you ever seen a group of mushrooms growing in a circle? People used to think that fairies and elves gathered each night in these circles, called fairy rings, to dance and play. Others believed that gnomes buried treasure in the rings. The circle of mushrooms really marks the outer edge of a spreading colony of fungi. The centre is bare because the food there has all been used up. The familiar mushroom you see sticking out of the ground or growing from damp, rotting wood is only one part of a larger fungus. The mushroom is the fruiting part of a fungus; it contains tiny spores to produce new fungi, like flowers contain seeds to produce new plants. The rest of the fungus is made of hyphae, which are root-like threads that spread underground or through rotting wood, sometimes for kilometres (miles). They absorb nutrients that help the fungus grow.

Because mushrooms need lots of moisture to grow, wetlands are perfect habitats for them. If you hike through a swamp or wooded bog after a rain, you'll find a rainbow of colourful fungi in all shapes and sizes.

TRY THIS! *Spore prints*

One way botanists (scientists who study plants and fungi) identify mushrooms is by their spores. Because spores are so tiny, the botanists examine the patterns and colours made by the millions of spores in each fruiting mushroom. You can make spore prints at home with some simple materials.

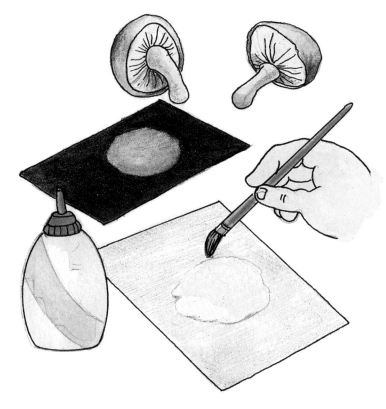

You'll need:
- a piece of white construction paper
- a piece of black construction paper
- white glue
- a small paintbrush
- gloves
- 2 fresh mushrooms of the same variety
- a knife
- 2 bowls
- fine, non-aerosol hairspray
- a field guide to mushrooms (optional)

1. Spread a thin coating of glue in a small circle on both sheets of paper. Lay the papers on a table, glue-side up.

2. Wear gloves when you handle unknown mushrooms, and never put them near your mouth. Cut the caps off each mushroom, close to the top of the stems. The gills are the feathery slits underneath the caps. Lay one mushroom gill-side down in the centre of the white paper and lay the other mushroom gill-side down on the black paper. Because you don't know whether the spores are light-coloured or dark-coloured, this will guarantee that a spore print will show up on one of the papers.

3. Place a bowl upside down over each mushroom and let them sit over night.

4. The next morning, remove the bowls and mushroom caps. Look at the colour of the mushrooms' spores and their patterns.

5. To preserve your spore print, spray it with a fine coating of hairspray.

6. Some field guides have spore-print charts, which may help you identify your mushrooms.

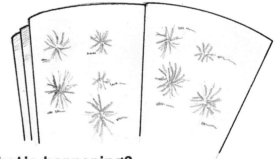

What's happening?
A mushroom's spores form on its gills and drop out of the mushroom when they are ripe and dry. Because the spores are so tiny, the wind easily blows them for many kilometres (miles), helping the mushrooms spread to new areas. With the protection of the bowls, your mushroom spores just fell straight down.

The spring chorus of frogs and toads

If you visit a marsh on a warm spring evening, you may hear what sounds like jingle bells or the twang of a loose banjo string. Your ears aren't playing tricks on you — you're actually hearing the sounds of frogs and toads. Every spring, hundreds of frogs and toads travel to the shallow water of wetlands to sing, mate and lay eggs. The males are the singers, who hope to attract female mates with their loud voices. Once you've heard a frog sing, you'll wonder how such a small animal can make such a loud noise. Male frogs and toads have a loose pouch of skin under their chin, called a vocal sac. Air is forced out of their lungs, through the throat and into the vocal sac, which puffs out like a big bubble. The leopard frog has two sacs — one on each side of its head. As the air passes through the throat, it vibrates the animal's vocal chords and produces the sound. To make another sound, air from the vocal sac is sent back to the lungs, once again passing over the vocal chords.

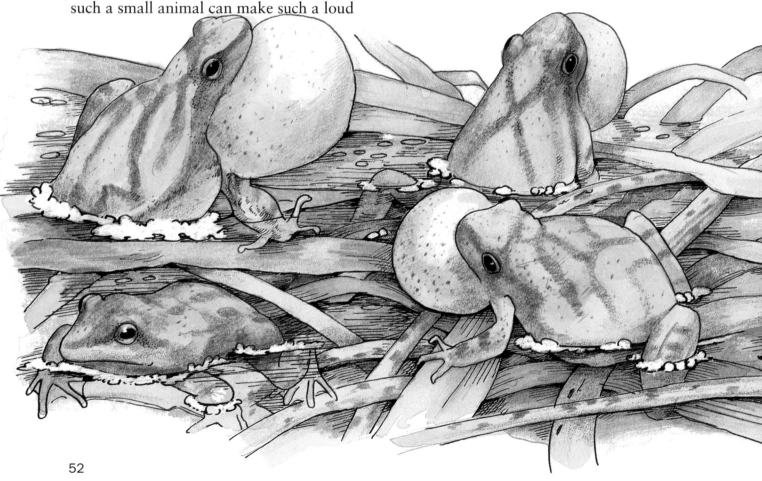

If you listen carefully, you'll be able to hear a variety of songs, depending on what kinds of frogs and toads live in the marsh or swamp you visit. Evening is the best time to hear frogs and toads sing. If you have a tape recorder, try recording their songs. Then play the recording back to the frogs and see (or hear) what happens. Here is a mini-guide to help you figure out who the singers are in your local spring chorus.

Singer		Song sounds like ...
Spring Peeper		sleigh bells
Green Frog		the twang of a loose banjo string, sometimes repeated rapidly
Wood Frog		a quacking duck
Bullfrog		a deep voice saying "chug-o-rum"
Northern Leopard Frog		a low, throaty snore of about three seconds, followed by clucking sounds
Chorus Frog		a fingernail running over the teeth of a comb for one to two seconds
American Toad		a musical trill lasting up to 30 seconds
Woodhouse's Toad		a nasal-sounding "baa-baa" of a sheep

Different ducks

Have you ever seen a duck stick its head underwater and its tail in the air, as if it's standing on its head? It's really just looking for food. Ducks that do this feed on plants or small animals at the water's surface or just below and are called dabblers or puddle ducks. Mallards and Black Ducks are common dabblers. Ducks, such as mergansers, that dive deep into the water in search of fish, small animals or plants are known as divers. You may think that all ducks look alike, but a closer look shows you how each one is specially adapted to catch and eat food in its own way.

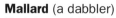

Mallard (a dabbler)
- [ ] No lobe on hind toe
- [ ] Legs set well forward on the body for balance on land and in water. (Dabblers can walk easily on land and can take off almost directly out of the water.)
- [ ] Usually a brightly coloured, iridescent wing patch
- [ ] A flat bill with special grooves that act like sieves, separating food from the inedible bits in muck

Common Merganser (a diver)
- ☐ Long toes with a broad lobe on hind toe — better for swimming
- ☐ Short legs set back on the body to provide speed and turning ability underwater. (Divers are very awkward on land and need to run or skim across the water to build up speed before takeoff.)
- ☐ No iridescent wing patch
- ☐ A shorter tail
- ☐ A narrow bill with sawtooth edges for catching and holding slippery fish. (Most divers have broad bills.)
- ☐ Streamlined body for swimming faster underwater

Wetland reptiles

The lazy, hazy days of summer bring out all kinds of sun worshippers, including turtles and snakes. These reptiles aren't working on a tan, they're raising their body temperature. Reptiles are cold-blooded. This means that their body temperature goes up and down depending on the temperature outside. So in cold weather a turtle's body is colder than it is in warm weather. Mammals, including you, are warm-blooded. A mammal keeps a constant, high body temperature except in the most extreme weather conditions.

You like to be warm to feel comfortable, but warming up is important for many other reasons too. Like mammals and birds, reptiles

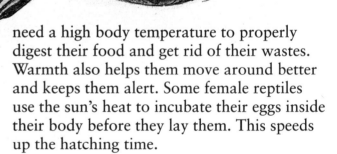

Water snake

Painted Turtle

need a high body temperature to properly digest their food and get rid of their wastes. Warmth also helps them move around better and keeps them alert. Some female reptiles use the sun's heat to incubate their eggs inside their body before they lay them. This speeds up the hatching time.

Basking in the sun is one of the best ways for reptiles to warm up. Use a pair of binoculars to look for sunning turtles on logs and rocks in the shallow water of marshes and bogs. You can find snakes lying in the sun on open paths or rocks in swamps, bogs and fens. You may even see a water snake swimming through the reeds in a marsh.

Warm-up exercise

You can discover the sun's warming ability for yourself. Choose two similar stones; place one in the sun and one in the shade. After a couple of hours, feel each stone. The one in the sun will feel hotter because it has absorbed heat from the sun, just as a reptile's body absorbs heat to raise its body temperature.

Dinosaur days

Did you know that dinosaurs were a kind of reptile? Turtles and lizards, which are also reptiles, first appeared on Earth about 200 million years ago — even before the dinosaurs' time. Some scientists believe that snakes slowly developed from ancient lizards about 100 million years ago. Snakes, turtles and lizards lived alongside dinosaurs, but they did not become extinct like their dinosaur relatives.

Although there are many theories about why dinosaurs became extinct, one popular belief is that Earth became colder. As it became chillier, many of the big reptiles — especially dinosaurs — could not keep their body temperatures high enough to stay active, so they died. Reptiles such as snakes, lizards and turtles could stay warm by burrowing into the ground, sheltering under rocks or moving to warmer seas. This is thought to have given them a better chance of surviving the cold weather.

How to set up an aquarium

What do you see when you look out your window? If you live in the city, you may see power lines, tall buildings and people. A window in the country might look out to farms, lakes and trees. Imagine what you'd see through an underwater wetland window: plants, insects, fish and other exciting creatures. With these instructions you can set up a clean and healthy aquarium — your own wetland window. Then read on to find out what amazing wetland creatures you can bring home to watch for a while.

You'll need:
- a glass aquarium tank
- clean gravel (from a pet store or garden centre)
- small stones
- marsh water (from the same marsh as the animals that you bring home)
- a large bucket
- aquatic plants such as elodea, pondweed or water plantain (from a marsh or pet store)
- a strainer (tied to a broom handle for a longer reach)
- waterproof plastic bags
- twist ties
- a piece of paper
- a thermometer

1. Put your aquarium out of direct sunlight, preferably near a north-facing window. Once you've added the water, use a thermometer to check that the water temperature does not get higher than 21°C (70°F).

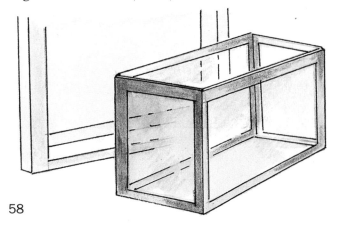

2. Wash the gravel and stones with water to clean off any dirt or hidden bacteria that could pollute your water. Place 5–10 cm (2–4 inches) of gravel over the bottom of the aquarium.

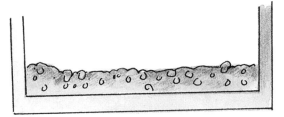

3. Collect enough clear marsh water in your bucket to fill your tank three-quarters of the way to the top. Choose a few aquatic plants (submerged and floating), scoop them up with your strainer and place them in water-filled plastic bags sealed with twist ties.

4. At home, lay a piece of paper over the gravel before pouring the marsh water into your tank. The paper will keep the gravel from being disturbed.

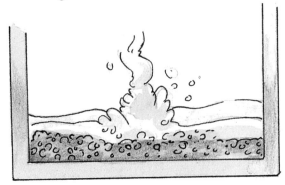

5. Remove the paper and add the plants to the aquarium, using small stones to anchor the submerged plants in the gravel.

6. Your aquarium is now ready for some marsh animals. You can use this temporary home to watch a variety of creatures from fish to frogs. See pages 60 to 73 to discover how to safely observe and take care of a variety of marsh life for a short time. Remember, if any of the animals you bring to your aquarium do not thrive, return them immediately to their original wetland home.

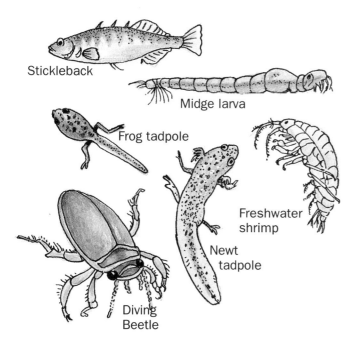

Stickleback

Midge larva

Frog tadpole

Freshwater shrimp

Newt tadpole

Diving Beetle

What if ...

... the water turns green? The green colour comes from too much algae, which are tiny water plants (see page 28). Add one or two pond snails from a marsh or pet store to your aquarium. They will eat the algae that grows on the glass. A sheet of dark paper taped onto the sunny side of the aquarium will block out some of the sunlight and slow down the growth of algae.

... some plants die? Remove dead plants so they don't make the water dirty. If your plants don't look healthy, check your water temperature to make sure it is not too high. Try moving your aquarium to a different spot to see if the plants improve. An air pump from a pet store will keep the water full of oxygen and may help the plants grow.

... the water level drops? Water will evaporate naturally from your aquarium. Fill up the tank to its original level every few days with fresh marsh water. Tap water can be used if it is left to sit in an open bucket for at least 24 hours to allow the chlorine to escape. Water straight from the tap can kill your marsh life.

... the water gets dirty? Scoop out half of your marsh water with a cup and replace it with fresh marsh water every week or so. If you are keeping animals that feed on plankton, such as tadpoles or insects, you should change the water twice a week to provide a fresh supply of plankton.

TRY THIS! *Fish watching*

Now that you have your aquarium set up (see pages 58–59), you're ready to bring home a wetland creature to watch for a while. Head to your nearest marsh to catch a few minnows or other small fish and bring them home to your aquarium. Be sure to check your local fish and wildlife regulations for information on what species can be netted legally.

You'll need:
- an aquarium set up as shown on pages 58—59
- a plastic bucket
- marsh water
- a small-mesh fishnet
- a few small fish
- food for fish: bloodworms, chopped mealworms, daphnia or insect larvae (from a pond or pet store)

1. Set up your aquarium as shown on pages 58–59.

2. Fill your bucket halfway to the top with marsh water and put it in the shade. Use your net to catch two or three small fish and place them immediately in the bucket. Take the fish home right away and put them in your prepared aquarium.

3. Wait a few days before feeding the fish to let them adjust to the aquarium. Feed your fish two or three times a week. Remove any food that isn't eaten in five minutes — any leftovers will rot, fouling up the water.

4. If the fish are gulping at the surface, they need more oxygen in the water. Add a few more aquatic plants, which release oxygen into the water. Fish kept for a long time need an aerator in the aquarium to pump oxygen into the water.

5. Watch your fish to see how they move, feed, breathe and react to danger. After a couple of weeks, release your fish back into the marsh, or sooner if they don't seem to be thriving.

Fancy fins and sensitive scales

If you look underneath a sailboat, you'll see a triangular shape called a keel sticking down into the water. The keel helps keep the boat from rolling over in the water. The pelvic fin, on the underside of a fish, works like a keel. The dorsal fins, which stick up from a fish's back, also help keep it upright in water. Watch your fish as they swim in the aquarium. Can you figure out what the side fins (pectorals) and the tail (caudal fin) are used for? Pectorals help a fish balance and turn, while the caudal fin is important for steering and propelling fast fish through the water.

Put a pencil into the water in front of a fish and watch what happens. The fish will swim away to avoid the obstacle, even if it doesn't see it. That's because fish can detect

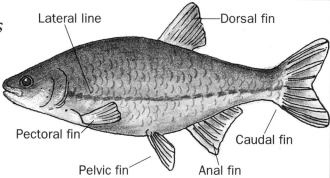

movements and changing currents in the water. On the sides of a fish's body, you can see a special line made up of scales that are a different shape from all of the other body scales. This is the lateral line. Beneath the lateral line is a very sensitive system of nerves that enable the fish to sense movement in the water.

Moving mouths

Have you ever wondered why fish always look like they are talking underwater? Fish open and close their mouths while they swim, in order to breathe. To get oxygen, a fish gulps water into its mouth and then pumps it out through slits at the sides of its head, called opercula, or gill covers. Look for the flapping gill covers on your fish. Beneath the gill covers are a fish's feathery gills. These act like lungs, taking oxygen from the water and releasing carbon dioxide. To stay alive, fish must keep fresh water constantly flowing over their gills, even while they're asleep!

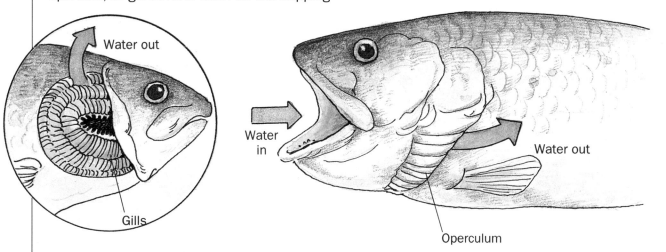

Saltwater fish

Wetlands on the shores of lakes and rivers contain fresh water, but wetlands along the coasts of the ocean contain salt water from the sea. Plants and animals living in coastal wetlands are specially adapted to surviving in salt water. For instance, fish in saltwater wetlands drink a lot of water to keep from drying out. The fish drink so much because water continually flows out of their bodies due to water's natural tendency to move towards saltier water. This process is called osmosis. Osmosis occurs when water flows through a barrier (such as a fish's skin) towards water that has more solid particles in it — in this case, the solids are salt. Although a fish's body naturally contains a small amount of salt, there is more salt in the wetland water, so the water flows out. In order to survive, fish living in a saltwater wetland continually drink water and hardly ever urinate. All of the extra salt they drink is let out through their gills.

Fish living in freshwater wetlands face the opposite challenge. The natural amount of salt in their bodies is higher than in the wetland water, so the fresh water moves *into* their bodies by osmosis. To compensate for this, and to avoid swelling up like a balloon, freshwater fish never drink and urinate often.

You can see how osmosis works with this simple experiment.

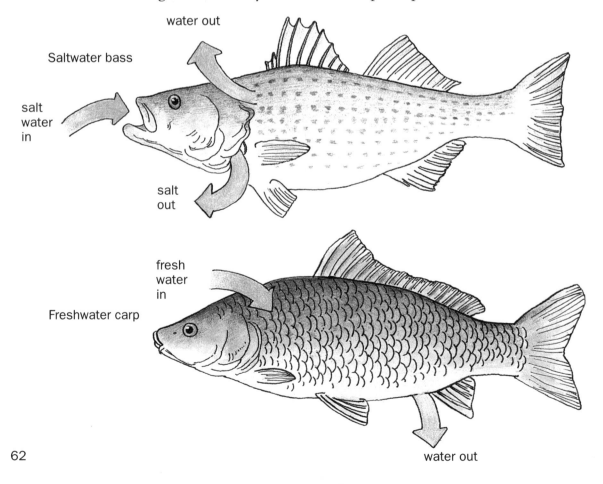

water out

Saltwater bass

salt water in

salt out

fresh water in

Freshwater carp

water out

You'll need:
- 10 raisins
- a glass of water
- a measuring cup
- water
- 2 shallow bowls
- a spoon
- salt
- a label (paper and tape will do)
- a pen
- a fresh cucumber
- a knife

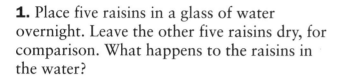

1. Place five raisins in a glass of water overnight. Leave the other five raisins dry, for comparison. What happens to the raisins in the water?

2. Pour 250 mL (1 cup) of water into each bowl. Add a spoonful of salt to one bowl. Label this bowl "salt." Stir the contents until the salt dissolves.

3. Carefully cut eight slices of cucumber. Feel the cucumber slices with your fingers and try bending them gently. Float four slices in each bowl. Leave the bowls for 45 minutes.

4. Take the cucumber slices out of the bowl of salt water. How do they feel now? How do the slices from the bowl of plain water feel?

What's happening?

The raisins in the glass absorbed water and swelled up because of osmosis. The water moved into the raisins because they were dry and contained more sugar than the surrounding water. Freshwater fish would swell up like raisins, too, if they didn't constantly get rid of their extra water. The cucumber slices left in the salt water feel limp because osmosis caused water to flow out of the cucumber slices into the surrounding salt water. This is similar to what happens to a fish in salt water. To replace its lost water, a saltwater fish drinks lots of water. The cucumbers in the plain water stayed fresh and firm because no osmosis took place.

Wetland Wildlife up Close

Whether you watch the slow and steady snail or the bustling beaver, you'll find that the pace of life in a wetland never stops. Take a day-hike to look for muskrat mounds and watch a heron fish, or go out in the evening to watch the swoops and dives of hunting bats. There's lots to do at home, too. Discover the fascinating life cycles of frogs and damselflies by raising them in your aquarium. You can even bring home some leeches for a few days to learn more about these amazing creatures that lurk under rocks in the mud. So turn the page and get a look at wetland wildlife up close.

Find out about frogs

Have you ever seen tiny, black, fish-like tadpoles swimming around in the shallows of marshes and ponds? In the summer, you can find all sorts of tadpoles — some with no legs and some with as many as four, some with long tails and some with short ones. Once all four legs are grown and the tail disappears, the tadpole also disappears — it has turned into a frog. You can watch the incredible life cycle of a frog in your aquarium over the summer.

You'll need:
- a small aquarium (set up as shown on pages 58–59)
- frog eggs
- a kitchen strainer
- a large plastic container with lid (a big ice-cream tub works well)
- marsh water
- a magnifying glass
- a cup
- food for tadpoles, such as lettuce and hard-boiled egg
- pieces of bark

1. Put your aquarium in a warm, bright area, out of direct sunlight. Set it up as outlined on pages 58–59.

2. You'll find the jelly-covered masses of frogs' eggs in the shallow waters of marshes and ponds, usually floating among plant stems. Scoop up some eggs with a kitchen strainer and put them in a large plastic container that is filled halfway with marsh water. Put the lid on your container and take it home immediately.

3. At home, transfer the eggs to your aquarium. The eggs will hatch two weeks after they were laid, releasing tiny, black tadpoles. Keep about four tadpoles and return the rest to the marsh.

4. Use a magnifying glass to see the tiny, feathery gills on both sides of a tadpole's head. The gills, tail and streamlined body make a tadpole look like a small fish.

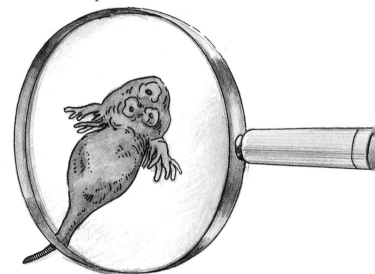

5. Tadpoles feed on tiny bits of algae in the marsh water, so you should change half of the water in your aquarium once a week to keep up the fresh supply of algae. Just scoop out half of the water with a cup and carefully pour in fresh water from the pond where you found the eggs. You can also feed the tadpoles small pieces of boiled or wilted lettuce or bits of hard-boiled egg every day. Use your strainer to clean out any uneaten food before adding more.

7. Four or five weeks after hatching, hind legs will appear, making the tadpole look part fish and part frog. Float some pieces of bark in the container so the tadpoles can climb out of the water.

8. About two weeks later, the front legs appear, growing out of the slits where the gills used to be. By the end of three months, all four legs will be fully developed.

6. Within a month, tadpole gills stop working because the tadpole has developed lungs inside its body. Notice how the tadpoles come to the surface for air instead of getting their oxygen directly out of the water, as before.

9. What is happening to the frogs' tails? As a tadpole turns into a frog, its tail gets shorter. The tadpole absorbs the tail, using the energy stored in it like food to help it grow and develop into an adult frog. Keep only one or two frogs and return the rest to the edge of the marsh. When the tails are nearly absorbed, transfer the frogs to an aquaterrarium. Turn the page to find out how to set one up.

Setting up an aquaterrarium

TRY THIS!

You'll need:
- a 19-L (5-gallon) aquarium
- clean, coarse gravel or sand
- bits of untreated charcoal
- soil
- small rocks and stones
- marsh water
- pieces of bark (found on the ground)
- net
- fine screening
- tape
- live food for adult frogs, such as mealworms or earthworms (from pet stores or bait dealers)

1. To make an aquaterrarium for the frog you've raised (see pages 66–67), place 5 cm (2 inches) of clean gravel or sand in half of the bottom of the aquarium and cover it with bits of charcoal for freshness. Add 10 cm (4 inches) of soil and keep the soil damp, but not soaked. Place some gravel over the edge of the soil where it slopes down to the empty part of the aquarium, to keep the soil from washing away. Add a few small rocks or stones.

2. Pour 5 cm (2 inches) of fresh marsh water into the empty side of the aquarium to serve as a mini-pond. Add some bark pieces to the land and water to give the frog some shelter.

3. Place the frog in the aquaterrarium using your hands or a net, and tape a screened cover over it to keep it from jumping out. Keep the container in a warm area, out of direct sunlight and where it will get lots of fresh air.

4. Unlike the plant-eating tadpoles, adult frogs eat meat and must be fed live food every day. You can buy food at pet stores or catch your own. Some frogs will eat bits of raw hamburger if it is placed on the end of a thread and jiggled in front of the frog as if it were alive. If your frog is not eating, return it to the wetland.

5. Watch your frog for up to a week and then return it to its marsh home.

Fast food

Frogs like fast food — not pizza but food that actually moves around! Flies are a favourite frog food. You know how hard it is to catch a fly with your hand. Imagine catching one with your tongue. Unlike your tongue, a frog's tongue is attached at the front of its mouth. When a frog sees food, it flicks out its sticky tongue, grabs the prey and pulls it back into its mouth. Frogs also have tiny teeth to hold onto their food before they swallow it whole.

Is it a frog or a toad?

Although frogs and toads look much the same, it's easy to tell them apart when you know what to look for.

A frog's mouth has small teeth to hold its food. Toads are toothless.

Frogs have slender bodies with smooth, wet skin. The round bodies of toads are covered with rough, dry skin.

Most frogs lay their eggs in water in clumps of floating jelly. Toads lay their eggs in long strings of jelly wrapped around underwater plants.

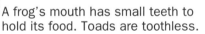

The long hind legs of frogs help them take large leaps and jumps. Toads have shorter legs for small hops.

You'll always find frogs living in or very near water. Adult toads may be found a long way from water.

TRY THIS! *Looking at leeches*

Here's an animal you can really get attached to. Or should I say it can get attached to you! Leeches are well known for their suckers that grab onto smooth surfaces such as rocks to anchor themselves in the water. Leeches also use their suckers to attach themselves to the bodies of fish, and occasionally to people, to suck their blood for food. Leeches come in different shapes, colours and sizes, ranging from as small as your fingernail to longer than your arm, but most are about finger-size. They live almost everywhere: in the Antarctic and in jungles, in deserts and on mountain tops, in water or on land. You can find leeches in wetlands among the plants in shallow, clean water, especially in spring or summer. Leeches prefer shady spots and often hide under rocks, logs or leaves.

You don't have to be stuck to a leech to get a close look at one. With some rubber gloves and tweezers, you can safely collect a few leeches, put them in a jar at home and watch these amazing animals as they swim gracefully through the water or climb, inchworm-style, up the sides of the glass. If you're only keeping leeches for a few weeks, you don't even have to feed them. That's because they eat so much in one meal, they can go for six months or a year without eating again.

You'll need:
- rubber gloves
- a kitchen strainer
- 3 or 4 leeches
- tweezers
- 2 plastic containers with lids (yoghurt containers work well) (one lid should have an air hole)
- some aquatic plants
- some cotton cloth
- clean marsh water or bottled spring water (not distilled water)
- small stones
- a large glass jar (a 4-L (1-gallon) condiment jar works well) or a small fish bowl or aquarium
- an elastic band or tape

1. Put on your rubber gloves. Check for the dark-coloured, worm-like leeches swimming in the shady areas of a marsh. Leeches may also be found hiding under small rocks or bits of wood. Gently scoop up a few with your strainer. Use your tweezers to transfer the leeches into a plastic container filled with damp water plants.

2. Place a cloth over the container and put the lid with the air hole cut out of it on the container. The cloth lets air into the container through the hole but keeps the leeches from escaping.

3. Collect some clean marsh water in your second plastic container to use in your jar at home, or use bottled spring water.

4. At home, place some stones in the bottom of your jar and add a few centimetres (an inch) of marsh water. Leave about 12 cm (5 inches) of air space between the water and the jar lid because some species of leeches like to attach themselves to the sides of the jar above the waterline.

5. Put the water plants in the jar. Then gently add the leeches to the jar with tweezers. Cover the jar with cloth and secure it with an elastic band. Leeches are great escape artists, so keep the jar covered all the time.

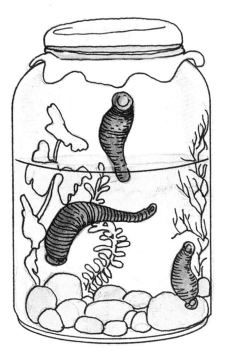

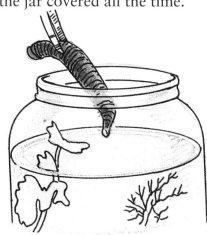

6. Place the jar out of direct sunlight or direct light from lamps. Leeches prefer the dark and are usually more active at night.

7. After a week or two, when you've finished looking at your leeches, carefully return them to the marsh.

What to look for

Look at your leeches carefully. Do they remind you of any other creatures? Leeches belong to the worm family and are close cousins to earthworms. Look for the faint lines that show you how the body is divided into sections. Like a worm's sections, a leech's sections can stretch out and squish up tight like a Slinky when it moves.

Leeches have tiny, coloured dots or patches along their bodies that are very sensitive to movement in the water. These help leeches find food. The dots are hard to see, but you can watch how they work by wiggling a plastic ruler or spatula in the water to see what happens. The leeches will sense the vibrations from the moving object and head for it, hoping to find food. If a leech attaches itself to the side of the jar, take a close look at its sucker-like mouth.

What to do if a leech latches on

Occasionally a marsh leech may latch on to a person. If this happens to you, you have a few minutes to get the leech off because it won't start feeding immediately. The best way is to flick it off with something stiff, such as a piece of plastic. Or you can gently squeeze its body until it lets go. As a last resort, sprinkle lemon juice or lime juice on the leech. This will make the leech drop off immediately but will likely kill it too.

When a leech bites, you usually don't feel it because a leech's saliva contains an anaesthetic that numbs your skin. The saliva also contains chemicals that keep your blood from clotting, so you may bleed a bit for about 20 minutes after the leech is gone. When a leech is full, it drops off by itself. Although a leech bite is unpleasant, it is not dangerous.

Snail watching

Having snails in a wetland is like having underwater housekeepers. Freshwater snails help keep the water clean by eating algae and decaying plants. Bring home a couple of snails from a local marsh for a few days and find out more about these slow and steady workers. They'll keep your aquarium clean, too.

You'll need:
- a small aquarium or 4-L (1-gallon) glass jar (a condiment jar works well)
- freshwater snails
- a kitchen strainer
- a plastic container with holes punched in the lid (yoghurt or margarine containers work well)
- some damp leaves from aquatic plants
- a large plastic container with a lid (a big ice-cream tub works well)
- marsh water
- some small, algae-covered rocks, including a piece of limestone (from the marsh or a garden centre)
- some fine screening
- tape or an elastic band
- a cup

1. Set up your aquarium or jar as outlined on pages 58–59.

2. Look for freshwater snails along the stems of aquatic plants or on the underside of the leaves. You may also find snails feeding on algae-covered rocks. Scoop a couple of snails up with your strainer and place them in a plastic container with some damp leaves. Put a lid with air holes on the container so the snails don't crawl out.

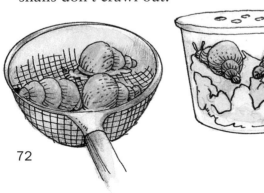

3. Fill a large plastic container with marsh water and take it home to fill your aquarium three-quarters of the way to the top. Add the small rocks you collected from the marsh. Snails also need a piece of limestone to help produce their shells.

4. Place the aquarium in a bright window and carefully transfer the snails to the aquarium. Cover the aquarium with fine screening and secure it with tape or an elastic band.

5. After a few days of snail watching, return the snails to the marsh. If you want to keep them longer, you need to replace half of the water in the aquarium with fresh marsh water every three days. This provides the snails with a new supply of algae. To change the water, simply scoop out half of the old water with a cup and slowly pour in the new water. Return the snails to the marsh by early fall.

What to look for

Watch how the snails slide up the sides of the glass on their muscular foot. Look for their slimy mucus trails that help them slide along. When a snail is feeding on the glass, take a close look at its mouth. Can you see its toothy tongue moving back and forth? A snail's tongue, called a radula, works like a file, rasping back and forth to shred its food.

You may see one of your snails travelling upside down, just below the water's surface. It looks as if it is walking on an invisible ceiling. Bend down and look through the side of your aquarium. At the surface, where the water meets the air, the water molecules "stick together" to form a strong, skin-like layer. This is called surface tension. This layer can support the weight of small aquatic animals. As the snail walks along the underside of the surface layer, its body is buoyed up by the water.

Snails are an important part of the wetland food chain. They feed on live plants, as well as break down dead and decaying plants to help recycle their nutrients. Snails are eaten by many wetland animals, including birds, fish and turtles.

Discovering bats

If you think bats only come out on Halloween, you should visit a wetland on a warm summer evening. At dusk, bats fly in open areas near trees and water, chasing their insect prey. Because wetlands are home to a lot of insects, they are great places for bats to hunt. To catch insects in flight, the skin between a bat's hind legs and tail forms a pouch that acts like an insect net. The trapped bugs are quickly eaten while the bat keeps flying.

Bats have an amazing ability to hunt and fly in complete darkness because they use sound to find prey and avoid obstacles. Bats produce sounds that bounce off objects nearby and then return to the bats' large ears as echoes. The echoes tell the bat the size and location of an object, as well as its speed if it's moving. This technique is called echolocation. You won't hear a bat hunting, though, because the sounds bats make are too high in pitch for people to hear.

During the day, bats roost in trees, caves, old mines and rock crevices. They usually hang upside down by their hind feet, which point backwards to help them hold on. In the fall, some bats migrate south to warmer areas, while others hibernate. Before hibernation, bats feast on wetland insects to get fat so they can survive the winter. Bats usually hibernate in caves and can be disturbed very easily. If you know where bats are hibernating, leave them alone until spring when you can watch them come out of their roost and fly around at dusk.

Bat watch

You can see echolocation in action with this simple trick. On a warm evening in summer or early fall, take a walk with an adult to a neighbourhood wetland, park or other open area surrounded by trees. Gather some woodchips or pebbles and throw them into the air above you, one at a time. Make sure there are no people around who may get hit. Bats flying nearby will detect the chips or pebbles with their echolocation abilities and will swoop in for a closer look, searching for food.

Holy bat trivia!

☐ Bats are the only mammals that can fly.

☐ In one summer, a hundred bats can eat over 2 million mosquitoes.

☐ The tongue of a nectar-feeding bat is one-quarter as long as the bat's body.

☐ The red bat has an average speed of 64 km/h (40 m.p.h.).

☐ Different kinds of bats eat insects, fruit, fish, nectar, rodents, frogs, blood and even other bats.

☐ The largest bats in the world are the flying foxes of Malaya, which have a wing span of 1.2–1.5 m (4–5 feet).

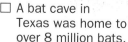

☐ A bat cave in Texas was home to over 8 million bats.

Muskrats in the marsh

What has a tail like a rat, webbed feet like a frog and teeth like a beaver? If you said a muskrat, you're right! These large, furry rodents are closely related to mice, rats and squirrels, but, unlike their relatives, muskrats spend most of their time in the water. The muskrat is an excellent swimmer, and its body is perfectly adapted to life in a wetland. Its partly webbed hind feet help the muskrat swim easily through the water, while its long, scaly tail acts as a rudder, steering the animal in the right direction. Two layers of fur — one short and thick and one long — provide a waterproof coat for the muskrat, keeping it warm and dry, both in water and out, all year long. A muskrat can even eat underwater. Its furry lips close behind its big front teeth to seal the animal's mouth. Then the muskrat can gnaw at submerged plants without getting water in its mouth.

How can you tell if a muskrat is living in a wetland? You may see a small, furry head poking out of the water as it swims through a marsh, or you may spot a line of bubbles left by a muskrat swimming under thin ice in the winter. But the easiest way to discover a muskrat is by looking for its mound-like house. Watch for muskrats building their homes in late summer or fall. Made from cattails or bulrushes, these dome-shaped houses are built on top of a log or stump, or in a clump of willows near deep water. The mound is plastered over with mud and pond weeds and may be up to 1.5 m (5 feet) above water level. Muskrat families stay snug inside their homes by sleeping on beds of dry grass. Muskrats travel under the ice to feed on underwater plants during winter.

As well as its home, a muskrat also builds several dome-shaped winter feeding stations called push-ups. When the first ice forms over the marsh, the muskrat chews a hole through a patch of ice, drags some underwater plants up through the hole and builds a dome with them, which completely covers the hole. The plants soon freeze solid and eventually become covered in snow. Every day the muskrat swims underwater to visit its push-ups and chews through any newly formed ice to keep the water hole open. The push-ups give the muskrat a sheltered spot where it can come out of the water to rest and feed, hidden from its enemies.

Marsh managers

While muskrats are busy cutting cattails and bulrushes for their homes or feeding on marsh plants, they're helping their marsh neighbours at the same time. By removing some of the fast-growing marsh vegetation, muskrats keep the plants from completely filling in open water or blocking the flow of water in streams and rivers. Open water is very important to the survival of other marsh animals, especially ducks. Ducks need clear water for landing and swimming. In some marshy areas, biologists have brought in muskrats from neighbouring wetlands to help control the spread of plants and to keep waterways from becoming overgrown or clogged up.

Beaver signs and sounds

People build dams to block the flow of water in a river or stream, in order to create lakes, control flooding or even produce hydroelectricity. Beavers also build dams that block the flow of water — their dams create ponds. A beaver needs a pond for many reasons, including shelter and food. It builds its home, or lodge, in the middle of the pond behind its dam, and uses the surrounding water like a moat to protect its house from enemies. Because every beaver needs trees for food and for repairing its lodge and dam, beavers flood land where trees grow. This lets beavers easily swim to the trees, cut them down and then float the logs in the water to their lodge, instead of having to drag them overland.

Beaver ponds not only give beavers a place to live, they also create new wetland habitats for lots of other wildlife including fish, mink, otter, moose, insects, frogs, turtles and ducks. In spring, when water from melting snow floods rivers and streams, a beaver dam can help hold back some of the flood water and slow it down. This helps stop the water from washing away stream beds and banks farther downstream. Too many beavers in one area can create problems, though, because they can flood farm fields or roads and can destroy many trees.

Dawn and dusk are the best times to go beaver watching in large marshes, wooded ponds, streams or rivers. If you don't see a beaver, keep your eyes and ears open, you may hear one instead, or see signs that tell you a beaver lives nearby.

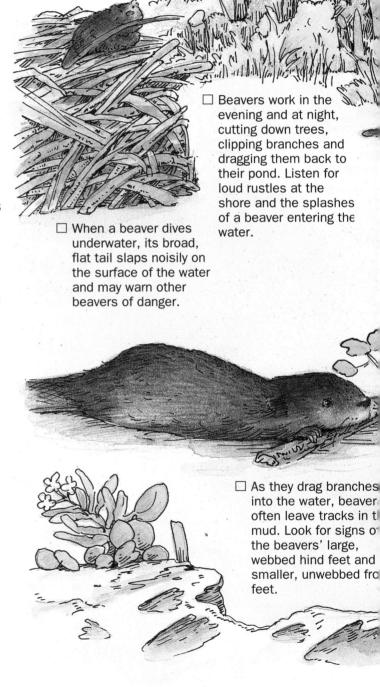

☐ Beavers work in the evening and at night, cutting down trees, clipping branches and dragging them back to their pond. Listen for loud rustles at the shore and the splashes of a beaver entering the water.

☐ When a beaver dives underwater, its broad, flat tail slaps noisily on the surface of the water and may warn other beavers of danger.

☐ As they drag branches into the water, beaver often leave tracks in t mud. Look for signs o the beavers' large, webbed hind feet and smaller, unwebbed fro feet.

☑ Lodges and dams may be made by one beaver or by a whole family.

☐ A dam is a sure sign of beaver activity.

☐ In large rivers, beavers make their homes in burrows dug out of the bank.

☐ Look for the dome-shaped beaver lodge made from mud and sticks.

☐ Along the shore, check for signs of chewed stumps. The beaver's chisel-like teeth leave easily recognizable marks on aspen, poplar, willow and birch stumps.

TRY THIS! *Raise a damselfly*

Dragonflies and damselflies have three stages in their life cycle: egg, nymph and adult. The eggs and nymphs live in water, but the adults live in the air and on plants surrounding ponds and marshes. In late spring, you can catch a damselfly nymph to keep in a jar of marsh water at home. There you can watch the nymph's amazing transformation into a beautiful adult.

You'll need:

- a large glass jar (a 4-L (1-gallon) condiment jar works well) or a small aquarium
- a kitchen strainer
- 2 or 3 damselfly nymphs (the largest ones you can find)
- 2 plastic containers with lids (large ice-cream tubs work well)
- marsh water
- food for the nymphs, such as small aquatic animals (mosquito larvae, waterfleas, small worms etc.) or mealworms (from a pet store)
- a long stick
- a turkey baster
- fine screening or cheesecloth
- an elastic band

1. Set up your jar or aquarium as shown on pages 58–59.

2. Use your strainer to scoop up some of the bottom muck from the shallows in a marsh or pond. Gently bob the strainer in the water. Look for any damselfly nymphs left in the strainer. They can be recognized by their long bodies, six legs and three tail-like gills that extend from their back end. Transfer two or three large nymphs to a container of marsh water kept in the shade.

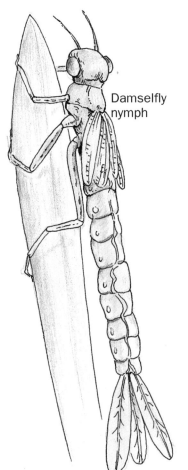

Damselfly nymph

3. Try to catch some other small aquatic insects with your strainer, especially mosquito larvae, to feed your nymphs. Place these in another container of marsh water and take both containers home.

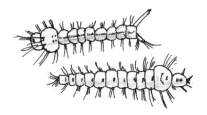

4. Fill your jar halfway with marsh water and add a stick that reaches high out of the water. Use a turkey baster to carefully transfer the nymphs to the jar. Cover the jar with fine netting or cheesecloth secured with an elastic band and place it away from direct sunlight.

5. Feed the nymphs every day with a few mosquito larvae or other aquatic animals, if available, or with some mealworms from a pet store. You'll have to make regular trips back to the marsh to get more aquatic insects.

6. Watch the damselfly nymphs for signs of change. As a nymph grows, it sheds its skin. In the morning, look for the see-through skins shed by the nymphs overnight.

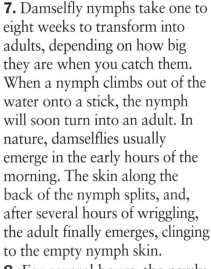

7. Damselfly nymphs take one to eight weeks to transform into adults, depending on how big they are when you catch them. When a nymph climbs out of the water onto a stick, the nymph will soon turn into an adult. In nature, damselflies usually emerge in the early hours of the morning. The skin along the back of the nymph splits, and, after several hours of wriggling, the adult finally emerges, clinging to the empty nymph skin.

8. For several hours, the newly emerged adult pumps fluids into its wings to stretch them out. At the same time, the soft wings and body begin to dry and harden. The damselfly's full colours don't appear for several days.

9. Once the adult is ready to fly (after about ten hours), release it in the marsh where you found it.

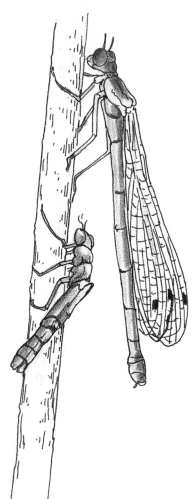

Dragonfly or damselfly?

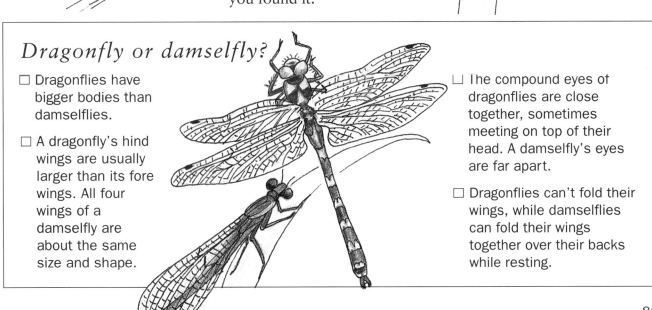

- ☐ Dragonflies have bigger bodies than damselflies.

- ☐ A dragonfly's hind wings are usually larger than its fore wings. All four wings of a damselfly are about the same size and shape.

- ☐ The compound eyes of dragonflies are close together, sometimes meeting on top of their head. A damselfly's eyes are far apart.

- ☐ Dragonflies can't fold their wings, while damselflies can fold their wings together over their backs while resting.

Getting to know Great Blue Herons

What's so great about Great Blue Herons? Plenty. From the tip of their dagger-like beaks to the ends of their long, skinny toes, these beautiful and graceful waders are remarkably well adapted to their life in wetlands. If you watch a heron stalking its prey slowly and silently in the shallows of a marsh, you'll see what a skillful and patient hunter it is. After eating a good meal, the heron spreads its huge wings and takes off with its feet dangling below like landing gear on an airplane. The heron is probably heading for its nest of sticks high up in the trees of a nearby swamp or forest. The Great Blue Heron is the largest and most common heron. Other herons to watch for in North American wetlands include the Green Heron, Black-crowned Night Heron, Yellow-crowned Night Heron, and the Little Blue Heron.

Although Great Blue Herons are large — some stand over 1 m (3 feet) tall — their size and shape help them blend in very well with the marsh vegetation. Read on to discover some of the other adaptations that make these birds so successful in their wetland habitat.

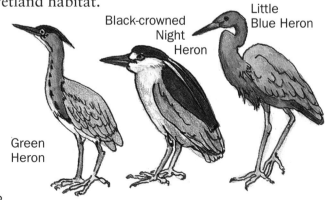

Green Heron

Black-crowned Night Heron

Little Blue Heron

☐ Look for the large, flat heron nests made from sticks. A group of three or four nests in the same tree is called a heronry. The tree trunk and the ground below heronries are usually whitewashed with the bird's guano, or droppings. Herons return to the same heronry year after year repairing and improving their nests each time.

☐ A long, flexible neck helps the heron dart its head quickly into the water in pursuit of food.

☐ The heron uses its strong, sharp beak to spear fish and frogs in the shallow water.

☐ Long, thin legs make it easy for the heron to wade through shallow water without getting its body wet. While hunting, herons often look like statues, standing still for many minutes as they wait for their prey to come close.

☐ The heron's long, skinny toes spread out on the muddy bottom for balance and to keep the bird from sinking in the mud. Because the toes are only slightly webbed, herons can still walk easily through the water as they stalk their prey.

Wetland Conservation

Now that you've discovered how important wetland habitats are for plants and animals, and how wetlands filter water and reduce flooding and erosion, you'll realize why wetlands need to be protected. Many wetlands have been polluted, drained for agriculture, filled in for construction or dug away to make waterways. Fortunately we are now starting to save our remaining wetlands through the co-operation of governments, conservation groups and people like you. Read on to find out how you can become a friend to wetlands. Then tell your friends, and they'll tell their friends ...

Saving our wetlands

Now that you've visited a wetland and discovered some of its amazing inhabitants, you know how important wetlands are to our environment. Wetlands have also played an important role in our history. The Native people of North America depended heavily on wetland plants and animals for food, medicine, clothing, crafts and tools. Early explorers and trappers knew wetlands as the source of furs; many trappers made their livings by harvesting beaver, mink, muskrat and otter. In fact, large areas of Canada and the United States were explored and opened up to settlers because of the fur trade in wetland animals. However, when the pioneers arrived, they often saw wetlands as mosquito-infested, dangerous areas. Because the wetlands could not be farmed, they thought of them as wastelands. Unfortunately, this idea that wetlands are somehow "bad" has been around a long time. We have drained wetlands, dug them out, filled them in and built on them because we did not understand how important wetlands are, both to their inhabitants and to us.

In some areas, such as parts of Ontario, it's too late to save most of the wetlands. Now there are no wetlands controlling spring flooding, filtering sediments and pollution out of the water, or protecting stream and river banks from erosion. The natural nurseries for fish, birds and other wildlife have disappeared. The loss of wetland habitats means there are fewer plants and animals; it also threatens species such as the Blanchard's Cricket Frog and the Spotted Turtle.

Many governments are now protecting special wetland areas by creating parks such as The Everglades National Park in Florida, Point Pelee National Park in Ontario and many smaller wildlife reserves and conservation areas across North America. We are finally working to save wetlands and make people more aware of their natural beauty and their important role in the environment.

As well as saving existing wetlands, some groups are actually restoring wetland areas. Many small prairie wetlands, called potholes, have been lost because of drainage and drought. Ducks depend on the potholes for food and nesting sites, and when the potholes disappear the ducks have nowhere to breed — they disappear, too. People from a variety of backgrounds are working together to restore wetlands where ducks can raise their young.

Prairie potholes

Importance of the wetland habitats

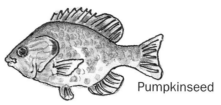

Pumpkinseed

This chart lists some of the larger animals that depend on wetlands for their survival.

Animal	Breeding	Feeding	Shelter	Totally Dependent	Partly Dependent
Mink	•	•	•		•
Otter		•			•
Painted Turtle	•	•	•	•	
Muskrat	•	•	•	•	
Beaver	•	•	•		•
Mallard (duck)	•	•	•	•	
Bald Eagle	•	•	•		•
White-tailed Deer		•	•		•
Great Blue Heron	•	•	•		•
Moose		•	•		•
Green Frog	•	•	•	•	
Pumpkinseed (fish)	•	•	•		•

Pollution problems

If the air in your home or the water in your taps were to become polluted, you would have to leave your home in order to survive. When the homes of wetland wildlife become polluted with oil or detergents from factories, houses or cottages, they must also leave, if they can. But insects, crustaceans, fish and aquatic plants can't leave and may die because of the pollution. Even larger animals will suffer if there is no other similar habitat nearby to go to. Try this experiment to find out how pollution can affect wetland wildlife.

You'll need:
- a clear glass bowl
- water
- cooking oil
- a spoon
- powdered laundry detergent

Part One
1. Fill your bowl halfway with water. Add two spoonfuls of cooking oil. The oil represents oil pollution in a wetland.

2. Stir the oil and water mixture with the spoon and then let it sit for one minute. Notice what happens to the oil in the water. Why do you think this happens?

What's happening?
The oil formed a separate layer on top of the water. This is because oil is lighter than water and it floats. In a wetland, a layer of oil acts like a barrier between the water's surface and the air above. Insects, such as mosquito larvae and other tiny animals that get their oxygen at the surface, can't break through the oil barrier so they suffocate. Animals that eat water plants that are covered in oil can get very sick.

Crude oil, the kind that sometimes gets spilled from ships at sea, is thicker and blacker than the cooking oil used in this experiment. It's also much heavier than the natural oils found on animals' fur and feathers. Birds such as terns and Belted Kingfishers, which dive from the air into the water to catch fish, can get covered with the sticky, heavy oil and then can't fly. The animals can be poisoned as they try to clean themselves by preening their feathers or licking their fur.

Part Two

1. Using your bowl of oil and water from Part One, sprinkle a spoonful of detergent into the bowl. The oil now represents the natural oils on a duck's feathers or on an aquatic mammal's fur, such as an otter. The detergent represents detergent pollution in a wetland. Stir the mixture gently, but not enough to create bubbles. Let the mixture sit for one minute. What happens to the oil? Where is the detergent?

What's happening?

When the detergent was added to the oil, the oil broke up into tiny droplets surrounded by detergent particles. Some of the oil may have even sunk to the bottom. The detergent connected the oil and water, causing them to mix together so that the oil and water no longer formed separate layers.

A duck's feathers have a natural coating of oil on them, like a protective cover. This makes the feathers waterproof and keeps the duck warm and dry while it swims in the water. When the water becomes polluted with detergent, the coating of oil on a bird's feathers is broken up into droplets, and water can get through to the feathers. If the feathers get soaked, the bird becomes cold and very wet. Wet feathers also make the bird much heavier — it can sink and drown. Aquatic mammals may also lose their natural waterproofing, in which case they become cold and wet and may die.

Endangered wetlands

This game will help you understand why wetlands are endangered habitats, and what is being done to protect them.

You'll need:
- 2–4 players
- a different-coloured button for each player
- one die

How to play:

1. Each button represents a wetland animal in search of a new home. Choose which animal you want to be.

2. Place your buttons in the start position.

3. Have each player roll the die in turn. The player with the highest number goes first, then the second highest and so on.

4. Move your button along the squares according to the number you roll. When you land on a "Thumbs Up" or "Thumbs Down" square, follow the instructions.

5. The first player (animal) to reach the wetland wins.

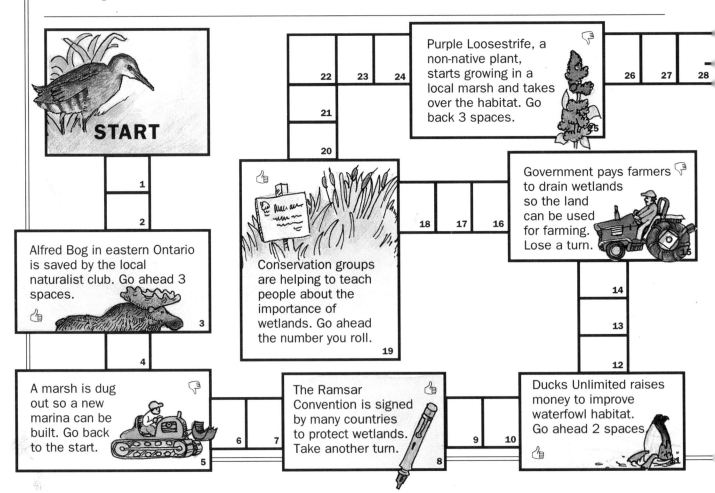

START

Alfred Bog in eastern Ontario is saved by the local naturalist club. Go ahead 3 spaces.

Purple Loosestrife, a non-native plant, starts growing in a local marsh and takes over the habitat. Go back 3 spaces.

Government pays farmers to drain wetlands so the land can be used for farming. Lose a turn.

Conservation groups are helping to teach people about the importance of wetlands. Go ahead the number you roll.

A marsh is dug out so a new marina can be built. Go back to the start.

The Ramsar Convention is signed by many countries to protect wetlands. Take another turn.

Ducks Unlimited raises money to improve waterfowl habitat. Go ahead 2 spaces.

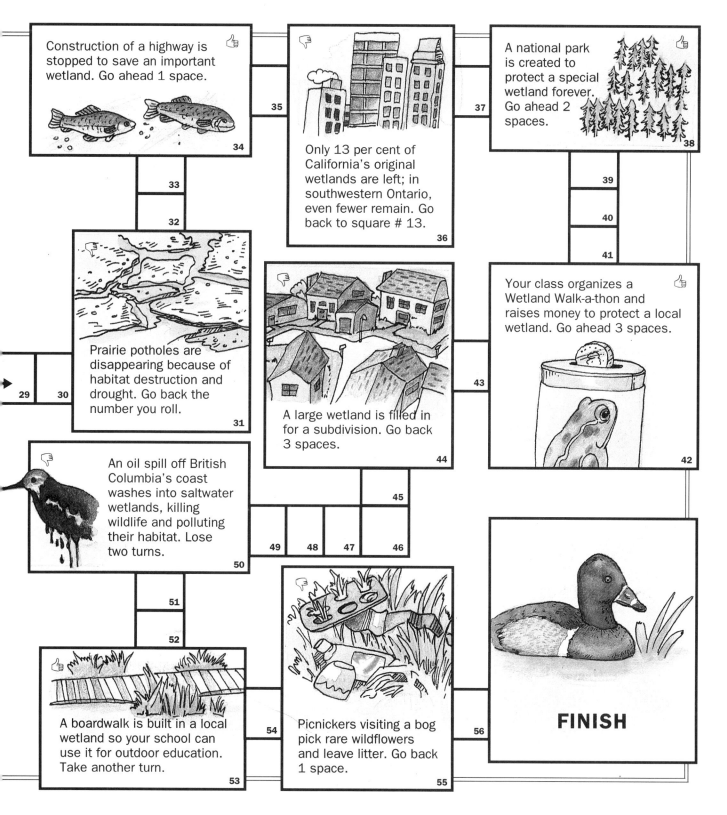

Construction of a highway is stopped to save an important wetland. Go ahead 1 space.

34

33

32

Only 13 per cent of California's original wetlands are left; in southwestern Ontario, even fewer remain. Go back to square # 13.

36

35

A national park is created to protect a special wetland forever. Go ahead 2 spaces.

38

37

39

40

41

Prairie potholes are disappearing because of habitat destruction and drought. Go back the number you roll.

31

29 **30**

A large wetland is filled in for a subdivision. Go back 3 spaces.

44

43

Your class organizes a Wetland Walk-a-thon and raises money to protect a local wetland. Go ahead 3 spaces.

42

45

49 **48** **47** **46**

An oil spill off British Columbia's coast washes into saltwater wetlands, killing wildlife and polluting their habitat. Lose two turns.

50

51

52

A boardwalk is built in a local wetland so your school can use it for outdoor education. Take another turn.

53

54

Picnickers visiting a bog pick rare wildflowers and leave litter. Go back 1 space.

55

56

FINISH

Wetlands and you

You've read about why wetlands need to be protected, so read on to find out how you can become a friend of the wetlands.

1. Get to know a local wetland. Visit it with a friend and find out what plants and animals live there. Watch how your wetland changes through the seasons. What roles does it play in the environment and in your community?

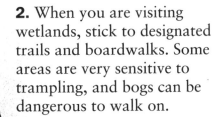

2. When you are visiting wetlands, stick to designated trails and boardwalks. Some areas are very sensitive to trampling, and bogs can be dangerous to walk on.

3. Contact the local government office in charge of natural resources and the environment to find out what laws exist in your area for the protection of wetlands. If there are no laws, write to your town council and your local member of parliament. Tell them why you think wetlands are important and how you think they should be protected.

A beautiful enemy to the wetlands

Have you seen the beautiful flowers of Purple Loosestrife growing in wetlands near you? These flowers are bad news for wetlands. Purple Loosestrife is a non-native plant to North America. This means that it doesn't grow naturally in the wild here. It is spreading quickly through our wetlands and taking over the habitat of plants that are naturally found there, such as reeds and cattails. This not only endangers the native wetland plants, but the animals that depend on those plants for food and shelter are suffering, too.

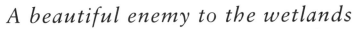

Biologists are experimenting with a natural way to prevent the Purple Loosestrife from spreading any more. They have discovered some Purple Loosestrife-eating beetles and are planning to release the beetles in wetlands where Purple Loosestrife is growing. This method of using nature to control a natural pest is called biocontrol.

In some wetlands, they are even trying to pull the Purple Loosestrife out by hand. If this is tried in a wetland near you, volunteer to lend a helping hand.

4. Join a conservation group that is working for wetland protection. Volunteer your time to help

5. Raise money for wetland protection. Be creative and get your class involved. Bake sales, car washes, raffles and fun fairs are all good ideas. Use a wetland theme to focus people's attention on your cause.

6. Organize a tour of a local wetland led by a good naturalist who will introduce people to the wonders and importance of wetlands. Invite your local media to come along (newspaper, radio station or television station).

7. Write to local newspapers and ask them to feature a story about the importance of wetlands in your community. Suggest people that they should talk to, such as local naturalists, canoeists, biologists (from a university, conservation organization or government office). You can also write a letter to the editor of your local newspaper, explaining how you feel about your local wetlands and how you would like the community to take care of them.

8. If your family owns property on a wetland at home or at a cottage, learn more about it and protect it. Ask your parents not to use harmful pesticides or chemical fertilizers on the property because they can be washed into the wetland. Don't mow or trample down the shoreline vegetation — it protects the shore from erosion and provides good habitat for a variety of creatures.

9. If you're camping near a wetland, remember not to litter. Avoid dumping phosphate detergents or other harmful substances into the water; use biodegradable, phosphate-free dish soaps, shampoos and body soaps.

Index

Answers

Camouflage in a wetland, pages 30 – 31

Water snake

American Bittern

Sora Rail

Marsh Wren and nest

Mink

Eastern Spiny Soft-shelled Turtle

Damselfly

Catfish

Caddisfly larva in case

Bullfrog

Wetlands at night, page 38

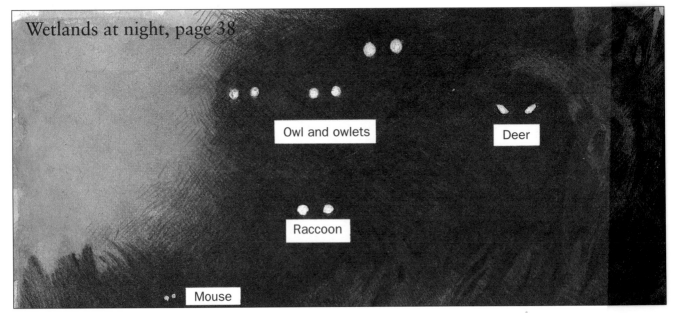

Owl and owlets

Deer

Raccoon

Mouse